PROF. GEORGE ZAFIROPOULOS

# FROM
# BACK
# PAIN
# TO
# PRODUCTIVITY

## A Business Leader's Guide
## Supporting Employees

**Author:** George Zafiropoulos @2024

**Title:** From Back Pain to Productivity

**ISBN:** 978-1-0686737-0-2

**Category:** Health/Back Pain/Pain Management

**Publisher:** Breakfree Forever Publishing

## IMPORTANT NOTICES / DISCLAIMERS

The depicted experience may be considered atypical. Your background, education, experience, and work ethic may differ. This is used as an example and not a guarantee of success, as everybody is unique. Individuals do not track the typicality of their students' experiences. Your results may vary.

The contents of this training, such as text, graphics, images, and other materials, are intended for informational and educational purposes and not for the purpose of rendering medical or mental health advice. The contents of this training are not intended to substitute for professional medical advice, diagnosis, and/or treatment. Please consult your medical professional before making changes to your diet, exercise routine, medical regimen, lifestyle, and/or mental health care.

This is not a Medical Consultation or Medical Advice. This is a Guide to be followed, aiming to improve the quality of your life. You can keep all necessary material and discard what is not working for you.

Stories shared during the sessions of the modules are true experiences of mine personally or of people who had crossed paths with me during consultations many years ago, and no personal details are shared within the course that can make them identifiable to anybody.

*Within the contents of the book, you will find pictures and illustrations relevant to the text. In addition, there are some random ones. People may feel that they are out of context. These are there to help the reader go through the content, helping their Cognitive Ergonomics by using Biophilia (Bio = Life or Nature and Philia = Friendship, so in free translation, it is the Like or Love of Nature). This creates a more pleasant reading experience.*

# Contents

▶ **Introduction** 5

▶ **Chapter One:** Ergonomics 23

▶ **Chapter Two:** Range 60

▶ **Chapter Three:** Assistance 93

▶ **Chapter Four:** Serenity 115

▶ **Chapter Five:** Equilibrium 154

▶ **Low Back Pain Further Information In Brief** 187

▶ **Epilogue** 200

# INTRODUCTION

In today's fast-paced business world, the well-being of employees plays a crucial role in the success and sustainability of any organisation. There is a critical need for business leaders to take proactive steps in addressing and alleviating employee back pain. As organisations increasingly recognise the impact of employee well-being on overall productivity, this report emphasises the significance of empowering leaders to implement strategies and initiatives aimed at mitigating back pain issues among their workforces. Business owners, managers, and CEOs are realising the profound impact that employee health has on productivity and overall workplace morale. One common challenge faced by many leaders is addressing the issue of low back pain among their workforces.

Low back pain is a pervasive health issue affecting millions of people around the world. It is calculated that 10% of the global population is suffering from low back pain. It is a concern affecting a considerable number of employees in various industries, as it is estimated that 16% of employees in any industry are suffering from low back pain. It not only poses challenges to individual well-being but also imposes a substantial economic burden on businesses and healthcare systems.

Statistics indicate a concerning rise in the prevalence and incidence of low back pain globally. An overview of the prevalence and impact of low back pain provides insight into the magnitude of the issue. Sedentary work environments, poor ergonomics, prolonged sitting, heavy lifting and other activities in physically demanding occupations contribute to the high incidence and widespread nature of this health issue among employees. Recognising these factors is essential for leaders seeking to create a supportive and health-conscious workplace. Chronic back pain not only hampers personal well-being but can also lead to decreased job satisfaction and increased turnover rates.

Employee well-being is more than just a perk; it is a strategic investment in a company's success. Numerous studies have demonstrated a strong correlation between employee health high productivity, and organisational success. When employees are in good physical condition, they are more likely to be engaged, focused, and motivated. Conversely, untreated health issues, such as lower back pain, can lead to absenteeism, decreased productivity, and increased healthcare costs for both employees and employers. It is found that from the number of employees who are absent due to lower back pain, twenty percent will stay off work for a month andsix percent stay away for a year. On top of that only seventy percent backreturn to their previous positions, so thirty percent either change jobs or companies, with all the financial consequences that follow this decision. This is because the departure could be amicable but on the other hand could be the result of a legal action against the organisation.

Reduced absenteeism, increased productivity, and enhanced job satisfaction are among the many benefits associated with a healthy workforce. Leaders must recognise that investing in employee well-being is not just a moral obligation but a strategic imperative for sustainable business performance. Understanding this prevalence is crucial for designing targeted interventions and policies.

To address the issue of lower back pain among employees, leaders need to be proactive in creating a supportive and healthy work environment. This involves implementing ergonomic workspace designs, promoting regular physical activity, and offering wellness programs specifically designed to target back pain issues. By taking these measures, leaders can foster a culture of well-being that extends beyond traditional healthcare benefits. As leaders play a pivotal role in shaping workplace culture and policies, it is crucial for them to acknowledge the importance of employee health and well-being, particularly in addressing musculoskeletal issues such as back pain.

Leadership empowerment in relieving back pain starts with education and awareness. Leaders must be educated on the causes and consequences of back pain. Business owners, managers, and CEOs should invest in educating themselves and their teams about the causes of lower back pain and preventive measures. Additionally, they should foster a workplace culture that promotes awareness and understanding of preventive measures. Conducting workshops, providing resources, and encouraging open communication can create a workplace where employees feel supported and understood.

Tailored wellness programmes that focus on exercises, ergonomic improvements, and educational sessions can significantly contribute to reducing back pain. These programs should be designed with the specific needs of the workforce in mind. They must include fitness routines, stretching exercises, and educational sessions on maintaining good posture and body mechanics. By tailoring wellness initiatives to the specific needs of their workforce, leaders can demonstrate a genuine commitment to the health and happiness of their employees.

The successful implementation of these strategies requires a commitment from leadership. This involves integrating back pain relief initiatives into the organisation's overall wellness programmes, policies, and day-to-day operations. Leaders should champion these efforts, demonstrating a genuine commitment to employee health.

Finally, the result has to be monitored and measured. These metrics for success should include a reduction in reported back pain instances, improved employee satisfaction scores, and increased participation in wellness programs. Regular assessments can help leaders gauge the effectiveness of implemented strategies and make informed adjustments. But is it necessary now during recession to start educational programmes? These can add further expenses.

In my humble view, this is the best time for these programmes to be implemented.

Healthy and pain-free employees are more likely to maintain optimal productivity levels. By addressing back pain during a recession, businesses can mitigate the risk of decreased efficiency and maintain their workforce's ability to contribute effectively. Addressing employees' health concerns, including back pain-, demonstrates a commitment to their well-being. This, in turn, can positively impact morale and engagement.

In a recessionary environment where job security may be a concern, showing support for employees' health contributes to a more positive workplace culture. Managing employee health, including back pain, can contribute to cost savings in the long run. Although investing in preventive measures and wellness programmes incurs some upfront costs, it can help avoid more significant healthcare expenses associated with chronic conditions and long-term disability claims.

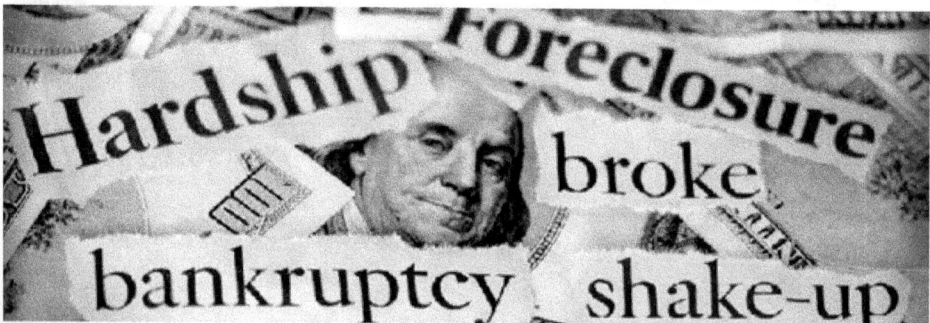

In a recession, businesses may be more competitive in attracting and retaining skilled talent. For every key-employee, it is found that a company spends an average of £4,000.00 pounds. Losing such persons is costing businesses money and productivity as they either overlook other teams or specialised machinery. A workplace that prioritises employee health and well-being, including addressing back pain issues, can be an attractive factor for potential employees and contribute to the retention of existing skilled talent. Ignoring back pain can lead to the escalation of health issues, potentially resulting in chronic conditions and more severe complications. Addressing back pain promptly can prevent long-term health problems, reducing the likelihood of extended medical leaves and disability claims; all of which are additional expenses that must be avoided during recession as every penny counts.

On top of that, healthy employees are more adaptable and flexible in their roles. This adaptability is very important, and I may add, very necessary during the financially difficult times. Addressing back pain allows employees to perform their duties with greater ease and flexibility, making it easier for businesses to navigate the challenges and changes that often accompany a recession. Neglecting employee health concerns, especially those related to workplace conditions and ergonomics, may lead to legal and compliance issues. Proactively addressing back pain aligns with occupational health and safety standards, reducing the risk of legal complications during a recession.

Companies that prioritise employee well-being, even during challenging economic times, can build a positive employer brand. This positive image can enhance the company's reputation and make it more appealing to both current and prospective employees.

So, dealing with back pain among employees during a recession is not only an investment in their well-being but also a strategic decision that contributes to maintaining a healthy, engaged, and productive workforce, even in challenging economic conditions.

In this book, we will explore the importance of empowering leaders to take proactive steps in relieving employee back pain. The positive outcomes of such action for both the employees and the organisation benefits, shed light on the multifaceted nature of the global lower back pain problem and explore potential strategies for mitigation. The global problem of workforce lower back pain is a complex challenge that demands a concerted effort from stakeholders across sectors. By prioritising preventive measures, implementing workplace interventions, and fostering international collaboration for education and training, we can work towards creating healthier, more productive workplaces that benefit both individuals and economies on a global scale. By empowering leaders to relieve employee back pain is not just a compassionate initiative but a strategic imperative for the success of any organization. By fostering a culture of well-being, investing in education, and implementing targeted wellness programs, leaders can create a workplace where employees thrive physically and professionally. In doing so, they pave the way for increased productivity, improved job satisfaction, and a stronger, more resilient workforce. As the business landscape continues to evolve, prioritising employee health will undoubtedly remain a cornerstone of effective leadership.

But who am I and what makes me qualified to talk about back pain?

I studied Medicine and later I specialised and became an Orthopaedic Surgeon. During my career I have seen and treated a great number of people who had suffered with back pain, so I have the understanding about the condition and the implications and effects to people's lives. I have been as expert witness in cases defending both employees and employers.

This though is not the only fact that makes me able to talk about the condition. I am or better was a severe chronic lower back pain sufferer. This change was because I managed to find ways to control the constant lower back pain and live a much better life now.

Due to an injury I had in the past, I have been suffering from chronic lower back pain and I am well acquainted with the meaning of "Back Pain". While I was at the acute phase of my symptoms, I really wanted information, answers, and support, as I believe everyone wants when an illness hits them. I am a chronic lower back pain sufferer and quite senior enough to understand all other limitations someone has and on top of that I have a total of over 42 years of Medicine, Science, Experience on my side and 39 years within Orthopaedic surgery.

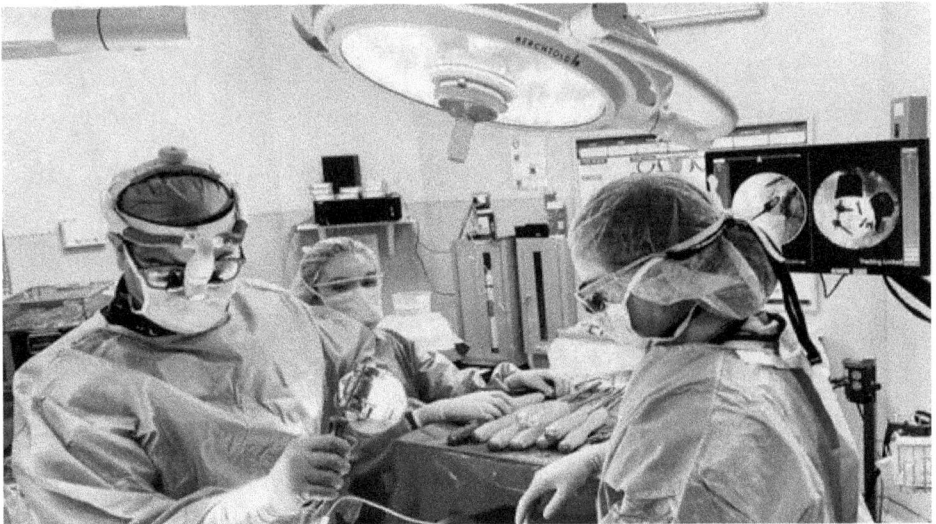

But let us clear up a few things. I believe universal agreement that every organisation is supported by their clients and the service the organisation is delivering to them. But how is this service is delivered? Who is delivering it? Have you ever considered that this can only be achieved by the work the workforce is providing? On top of this, there is also an agreement that for the provision of a service the employees have to be supported. But at what level can the organisation can stretch itself to support these employees?

Let me ask a question,.

How far are you willing to go to support your key staff?  How happy are you to provide to for them in your attempt to have happy clients and achieve greater productivity?

Do you think that the organisation could resemble a Swiss clock, where the gears of it are nothing more than the workers?

Why do I say a Swiss clock? Because you would like for your organisation to work in such precision and accuracy, achieving the optimal efficiency as the clock does in the attempt to show the correct time for ever. So, we must think about it.

Before this question could be answered, let's see it through the lens of my experience.

It all started one day in the operating theatre. I had to operate an acromegalic (giant in other words) patient. He was taller and longer than the operating table and his weight was more than 150 kilos (kg)-(330 pounds). After he was anaesthetised, we had to reposition and turn him to one side, in preparation for the operation.

A team of six people gathered around the operating table. The anaesthetist was on the top to control his head and neck. Four people on one side to do the initial lifting and myself on the other side to help the lift, pull, finalise the positioning and stabilise him with the supports, in the way it was necessary for the procedure.

Unfortunately, during the final moment of countdown, one member of on the opposite side of mye team changed position resulting to the whole disorganisation of everybodythe group. I was left alone to pull almost the entire 150kg. My spine "cracked" and felt pain running through the length

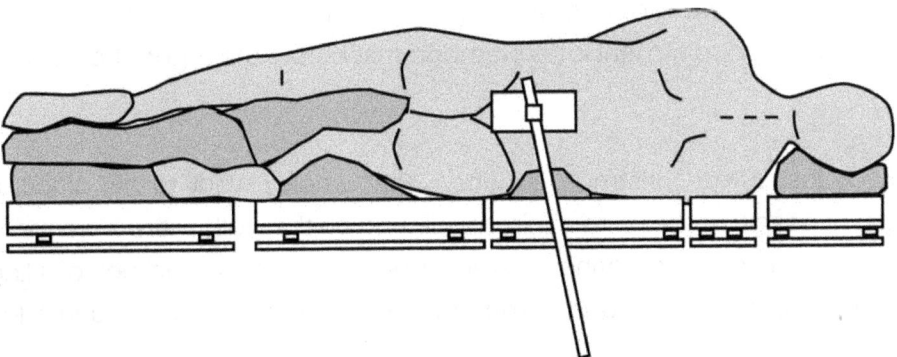

of it. It took me some time to straighten my body. I was given painkillers by one of the nurses and slowly I managed to come back to the upright position. I had to go ahead perform the surgery, as there was no other surgeon available to help and after I finished the operation, I threw myself face down on one of the theatre trolleys. More Additional painkillers were given to me and when I felt better, I drove home. That night I could not sleep, turning as I was trying to find a comfortable position. When I informed the Hospital in the morning about my pain and stiff back, I was told that a clinic already was booked for me, and they were unable to cancel it. There was nobody available to replace me, so I was called back on duty. This acute pain forced me to move in a tilted position. I went to my doctor who sent me for X-rays and gave me painkillers. The results of the radiological investigations came up as "there is no congenital deformity or fracture" something that I already knew. Following this, my doctor said that possibly all this was muscular, and he only provided me with painkillers and never sent me to physiotherapy or allowed me to stay out of duty.

The pain carried on for months and I was walking in pain and with a twisted back.  My doctor was saying to me that I am an oOrthopaedic sSurgeon and I know how to treat back pains better than him. There was a caveat; I could not self-refer to have any other treatment or investigation due to regulations and only he could offer such service by requesting or suggesting these alternatives. I called my manager for any help but they was were constantly busy and unable to take my calls.

About 4 or 5 months after that initial episode, I asked to see my manager and had an appointment late afternoon, just before the end of the working day.

It was just after Christmas, January 2004 when I went to his office, a regular hospital room with minimal painting on the wall.; There were more informative and promoting posters than paintings. A number of filing cabinets were around and some low comfortable chairs. I was in such a great deal of pain in my back and despite the empty chairs it was not possible for me to sit. Behind the desk in front of me, was a big man–John, my manager. Broad shoulders indicating the years he spent on rugby training. His face was always "dark" as he was not a usually a happy man. He was writing something on some papers and without lifting his eyes from the documents he asked the reason of my visit. I explained that in my opinion he had to help me and refer me to the occupational health as I had no luck with my doctor; and I was unable to refer myself to have any treatment. I explained that up to that time point as I was the only orthopaedic surgeon in the department, I had not taken any time off as I did not want to create any problems to hHospital's service but I could take if necessary.

He raised his piercing eyes and spat out:

"Are you threatening me? Do you want to face the disciplinary committee?"

MOn my reply was that this was not a threat but a possible necessity, he went back on the papers, waved his hand in a dismissive way and replied that he had no time for this, it was not his problem, and I was wasting his time. I was told that I had to find the solution of my problems. That's it. I was dismissed without him even looking me in the eyes, except the only second that he had to "throw fire" on me.

I chose not to take sick leave as this would create massive problems to the patients but I decided to do the minimum movement which resulted in a slow but steady increase of my weight. My mood was wavy following my pain's frequency wave pattern, matching exactly the waves of the pain's intensity. When my pain was increasing, my mood was decreasing and the opposite. Family life was affected because of my behaviour. Nobody was happy anymore, . Everybody was under stress. I was constantly worried and questioning myself if this will be my life from that time onwards. I believe the rest of the family had the same thoughts, but they were not voicing them. I was getting deeper and deeper into depression, driving everybody around me into the same dark place. In addition, my general health started to be influenced by the whole condition. I was not able to climb stairs anymore, I had lost stamina, I was getting breathless, and my blood pressure went through the roof. I was worrying about me but at the same time I had to look after my patients, adding extra stress on me.

Several months later and as I was walking to the hospital's restaurant still with a twisting and painful spine, a bigger sized body and slow pace I heard a voice from behind me, bringing me out of the pleasurable thoughts of a nice meal. The restaurant had a carvery roast today and it was really tasty.

"Hey George, is it you? What happen to you man?"

Who was this person? Who takes me out of the only pleasure that I had left; food and the thoughts of it?

Doing a full body turn I saw David, a tall and athletic slightly younger physician of mine and good friend. He commented on my weight as I had gained a lot of it and asked me about my health. I explained my situation, my inability to get any treatment, my inability to even tie my shoe-laces without holding my breath, my manager's attitude and the only pleasure I am left with, food! He asked me to go with him into the clinic. He examined me, took bloods, and asked me to come back to the clinic in-few days.

That second day in the clinic, he sat in front of me and told me that he will arrange physiotherapy, a decision that made me jubilant, but this euphoria was demolished as soon as he said that I am borderline hypertensive and may be close to a pre-diabetic status. If I was not ready to change my lifestyle, he would be forced to "feed" me more pills, of all kinds, to control my "issues" and this treatment would have to be for life.

"Me, I am a surgeon, a doctor, I hate pills. I don't take them". Those were my thoughts. That was the wakeup call.

Something kicked in my brain. I was not prepared to keep taking medications for life. When I refused his offer, he looked at me and gave me an ultimatum of six months to pull myself out of my misery. I had to change my body and my attitude. I had to decide in either accepting defeat and taking pills or control my health. I was in the depth of a dark valleyvalley, and I had to come out of it. I had to be "resurrected" by becoming free from all these troubles that had crossed my path and threw me into the abyss.

That was it,. I started my own research,. I studied numerous of papers and books. As nobody was prepared to help me, I had to help myself on my own. I went back to being reminded about metabolism in the physiology textbook, endocrinology, and finally chronic pain management. Following all this with a lot of trial and error I had successfully done it.

On top of this, I had a miraculous "accident" that made things "better". I was dictating a letter to my secretary after a long day's work. My back pain was not permitting me to sit on my chair, so instead I placed my one knee on the seat and held the back of the chair stabilising it, so I could rest from standing all day long. The chair was a rotating office seat and whilst talking suddenly lost balance and I twisted my back trying to avoid a fall. A sharp pain went through my spine and thise acute pain I had for months was disappeared. I was so happy, but over time I found out that it was replaced by a dull discomfort that became a constant presence. It was getting worse every morning. I had a stiff back, moving like a robot and with fmany limitations, unable to bend freely in any direction. The pain had ups and downs in frequency and intensity throughout the day, but it was present at all times. This resulted in periodic use of painkillers, which helped me cope with the symptoms. Despite this, I was determined to continue my plan for self-improvement.

Initially, I started moving. The initial short walks became longer and, slowly, I could walk miles and miles. I joined the gym, lost weight. My blood pressure and blood sugar went back to normal levels, and as my body became stronger, my dull back pain visiting me on rare occasions. My mood swings stopped, I became happier, and my family started to smile again. Saying all that, I stress to all of you, that I know what chronic back pain is. I went through it and conquered it.

It washad been almost a year since the visit to David's clinic and the ultimatum he had placed on the platter in front of me. I am back in the hospital's restaurant, and now instead of roast, I eat salad. I am longer called Papa Smurf, as this was my nickname in the theatre;. I have no difficulties running upstairs and definitely no issues to tying my shoe-laces. I have lost 30 kilos, and I am 99.9% symptom -free. You may ask, "Do you really fully treat back pain?" but mMy answer will be that back pain can only be managed, having a couple of days of pain every six months can be considered as "elimination" of the symptoms. Going back toTo answer the previous question, if you want your business to work like a Swiss clock, we need to answer another question. Do you want people like John, my manager, or people like David, my colleague, in your company? The answer may be obvious.

But how far are you willing to go to support your team? What mechanisms would you provide for them, and how would you implement them to make ensure that your employees are moving like a robot and with a lot ofmany limitations, unable to bend freely in any direction. The pain had the ups and downs in frequency and intensity throughout the day, but it was present at all times. This resulted toin periodically use of painkillers, helping me towhich helped me cope with the symptoms. Despite this, I was determined to continue my plan tofor self-improvement.

Initially, I started to movemoving. The initial short walks became longer and, slowly, I could walk miles onand miles. I joined the gym, lost weight. BMy blood pressure and blood sugar went back to normal levels, and as themy body became stronger, my dull back pain was visitinged me on rare occasions. My mood swings stopped, I became happier, and my family started to smile again. Saying all that, I stress to all of you, that I know what chronic back pain is. I went through it and conquered it.

It washad been almost a year since the visit into David's clinic and the ultimatum he had placed on the platter in front ofgiven me. I am back in the hospital's restaurant, and now instead of roast, I eat salad. I am not any more longer called Papa Smurf, as thisat was my nickname in the theatre;. I have no difficulties to running upstairs and definitely no issues to tieying my shoe-laces. I have lost 30 kilos, and I am 99.9% symptom -free. IYou may be asked, "Do you really fully treat back pain?" but mMy answer will be that back pain can only be managed, and to havehaving a couple of days of pain every six months can be considered as "elimination" of the symptoms. Going back toTo answer the previous question, if you want your business to work aslike a Swiss clock, we need to answer another question. Do you want in your company people like John, my manager, or people like David, my colleague, in your company? The answer may be obvious.

But how far are you willing to go to support your team? What mechanisms would you provide for them, and how would you implement them to make ensure that your employees are supported? How does an organisation act in an attempt to achieve better service for their clients while simultaneously increasing productivity and lowerreducing costs? How can an organisation keep its staff as healthy as possible? It is not necessary to spend time on big issues and plans, but rather to truly delve in and try to understand and find out what the needs of those small parts of the clock machine that move your company are. These parts are your employees. Managers take care of them, helping their company to be productive, expand and thrive.

Due to this life experience and being able to understand the situation, as well as my professional and scientific knowledge, I am able to serve others in overcoming the same problems by sharing the information and support, something that nobody provided to me when I needed it. I am ready to discuss the steps and strategies that helped me overcome this burden.

The E.R.A.S.E. Low Back Pain Formula is designed to provide you with the solutions and strategies that will help you understand people with back pain, care or them, and support them. These solutions and strategies are the "gears" that keep the business moving, and without this knowledge, your well-functioning Swiss clock may halt.

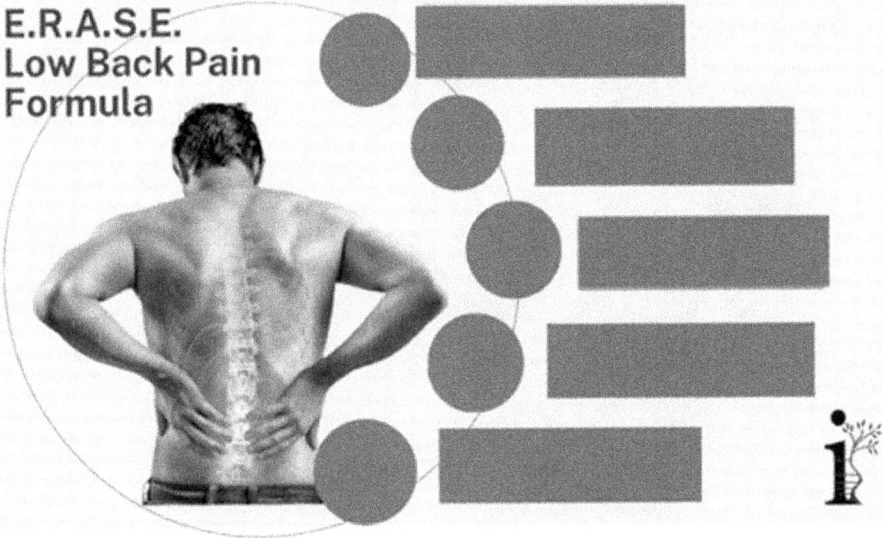

E.R.A.S.E.
Low Back Pain
Formula

I look forward to this challenge; I am ready to serve Bbusiness Lleaders and explain step by step the different aspects of low back pain and the relation with the company's approach to employee wellbeing by addressing both physical and mental health aspects. I will also explain how this can contribute to a healthier, more engaged workforce, ultimately enhancing overall productivity and job satisfaction.

This is my purpose; to help you move forward, to help you to come out of the misery, face back pain head-on, by recognising and accommodating diverse employee needs, including those with existing back pain. Companies that create inclusive workspaces and provide reasonable accommodations foster a positive and supportive culture.

Analysing the E.R.A.S.E. Low Back Pain Formula, you observe that the word E.R.A.S.E. is an acronym. What is the meaning of this? It means that every single letter of this word corresponds to a different entity. The letters correspond to Ergonomics, Range, Assistance, Serenity, and Equilibrium.

We will need to analyse one by one the different entities and the subsystems that they have within. A possible common observation will be that despite the different subsystems, there may be overlapping content between them. This is understandable as the subject to be tackled is Back Pain in the Workplace Environment, which may be considered multilevel but has an only single base: the Back Pain.

# 1
## CHAPTER

# ERGONOMICS

## ▶ But what is Ergonomics?

Ergonomics, also known as human factors engineering or human ergonomics, is the scientific discipline that studies the interactions between humans and their environments, with the goal of designing and arranging things to optimise human well-being and overall system performance. The primary focus of ergonomics is to create environments, products, and systems that are safe, efficient, and comfortable for human use. Within this discipline, there are other subcategories that may be useful to all or only part of you.

These key subcategories of ergonomics include:

- **Physical Ergonomics:** This involves designing workspaces, tools, equipment, and furniture to accommodate the physical characteristics and capabilities of the human body. Proper desk and chair height, keyboard placement, and monitor positioning are examples of physical ergonomic considerations.

- **Cognitive Ergonomics:** Cognitive ergonomics is concerned with mental processes such as perception, memory, reasoning, and attention. It involves designing tasks and interfaces that are cognitively efficient and reduce the mental workload on individuals. User-friendly software interfaces and well-organized information displays are examples of cognitive ergonomic considerations.

- **Organisational Ergonomics:** This aspect focuses on optimising the overall organisational structure, policies, and processes to enhance efficiency and employee well-being. Considerations include workload distribution, communication channels, and teamwork dynamics.

- **Biomechanical Ergonomics:** Biomechanical ergonomics studies the mechanics of the human body and its movements. It aims to design tasks and equipment that minimize physical strain and reduce the risk of musculoskeletal disorders. Proper lifting techniques and the design of tools to reduce repetitive strain are examples of biomechanical ergonomic considerations.

- **Environmental Ergonomics:** Environmental ergonomics involves the design of the physical environment to ensure optimal comfort and safety. Lighting, temperature, noise levels, and air quality are factors that can impact the ergonomic design of a space.

The overarching goal of ergonomics is to create a harmonious interaction between people and their work environment, promoting efficiency, health, and well-being. Proper ergonomic design can lead to a variety of benefits, including increased productivity, reduced risk of injury, improved job satisfaction, and enhanced overall performance.

In the context of workplaces, ergonomic principles are often applied to office furniture, computer workstations, manufacturing processes, and other aspects of job design to create environments that support the physical and mental well-being of employees.

First, let's dive further into physical ergonomics. This part focuses on the design and arrangement of physical elements in the workplace to ensure that they align with the capabilities and limitations of the human body. This aspect of ergonomics aims to minimise physical discomfort, prevent musculoskeletal disorders, and optimise overall well-being. So physical ergonomics can be analysed as:

a. **Workstation Design:** Proper workstation design is a fundamental aspect of physical ergonomics. This includes the arrangement of desks, chairs, monitors, keyboards, and other equipment to support a natural and comfortable posture for the user. Considerations such as desk height, chair adjustments, and monitor positioning are crucial to prevent strain on the neck, shoulders, and back.

b. **Seating Arrangements:** Ergonomic seating is essential for maintaining good posture and reducing the risk of back pain. Chairs should provide proper lumbar support, be adjustable to accommodate different body sizes and allow users to maintain a neutral and comfortable sitting position.

c. **Computer Ergonomics:** Computer workstations are a common source of ergonomic challenges. Physical ergonomics addresses factors such as the height and angle of the monitor, keyboard design, and mouse placement. These considerations help prevent issues like eye strain, carpal tunnel syndrome, and other repetitive strain injuries.

d. **Tools and Equipment Design:** Tools and equipment used in various work settings must be designed with ergonomics in mind. This includes the design of hand tools, machinery controls, and other equipment to minimize physical effort, reduce awkward postures, and prevent injuries associated with repetitive tasks.

e.  **Lifting and Material Handling:** Physical ergonomics is particularly concerned with lifting and material handling tasks. Proper techniques for lifting heavy objects and the design of equipment such as lifting aids contribute to the prevention of back injuries and musculoskeletal strains.

f.  **Repetitive Motion Considerations:** Repetitive motions, such as typing or assembly line work, can lead to cumulative trauma disorders. Physical ergonomics addresses ways to minimise the impact of repetitive tasks on the body, such as providing ergonomic keyboards, adjustable work surfaces, and implementing rotation of tasks.

g.  **Breaks and Movement:** Encouraging breaks and movement throughout the workday is an essential aspect of physical ergonomics. Designing work schedules that allow for regular breaks and incorporating ergonomic principles into break areas contributes to reducing fatigue and promoting overall health.

**h. Training and Awareness:** Encouraging breaks and movement throughout the workday is an essential aspect of physical ergonomics. Designing work schedules that allow for regular breaks and incorporating ergonomic principles into break areas contributes to reducing fatigue and promoting overall health.

**i. Health and Well-being Impact:** Proper implementation of physical ergonomics contributes to the overall health and well-being of employees. By reducing the physical stress associated with work tasks, companies can enhance job satisfaction, decrease absenteeism due to musculoskeletal issues, and promote a healthier workforce.

Physical ergonomics is a critical aspect of creating a workplace that promotes the health, safety, and efficiency of employees. By considering the physical aspects of the work environment and aligning them with human capabilities, organisations can reduce the risk of injuries, improve productivity, and enhance the overall quality of work life.

Next is Cognitive ergonomics, also known as mental ergonomics, is the branch of ergonomics that focuses on optimising the design of tasks, systems, and interfaces to enhance human cognitive performance. It involves understanding and improving mental processes such as perception, memory, attention, decision-making, and problem-solving.

Cognitive ergonomics plays a crucial role in the design of user interfaces for software, websites, and various technological systems. User-friendly interfaces with intuitive navigation, clear information presentation, and logical organisation contribute to reducing cognitive load and enhancing user experience.

Effective communication of information is vital in cognitive ergonomics. The design of information displays, whether on computer screens, dashboards, or in physical spaces, should consider principles such as clarity, simplicity, and relevance to facilitate quick and accurate understanding.

In complex environments, cognitive ergonomics is applied to the design of decision support systems. These systems aim to assist users in making informed decisions by presenting relevant information in a format that is easy to comprehend, reducing cognitive effort, and minimizing the risk of errors.

Cognitive ergonomics addresses the complexity of tasks and the associated cognitive workload. By understanding the cognitive demands of different tasks, organisations can optimise job roles, distribute workload appropriately, and prevent cognitive fatigue, ultimately improving performance and decision-making.

Designing training programs and educational materials that align with cognitive ergonomics principles facilitate efficient skill acquisition and knowledge retention. Interactive and engaging training methods enhance the learning process and reduce cognitive barriers.

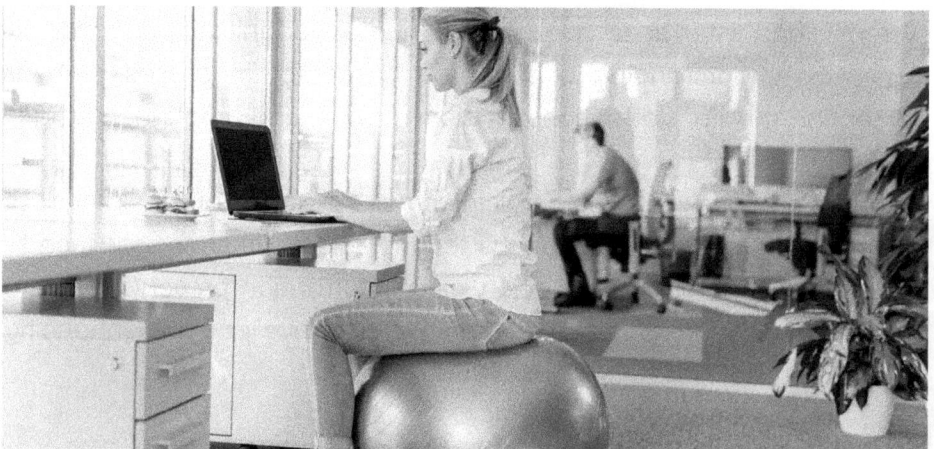

Cognitive ergonomics is crucial in human-computer interaction. It considers how users perceive, interpret, and respond to information presented by computers and devices. Designing systems that align with cognitive processes helps in creating a seamless and effective interaction between humans and technology.

Attention is a limited resource, and cognitive ergonomics involves strategies to manage attention effectively. This includes minimising distractions, prioritising information, and providing cues to direct attention where it is most needed.

Cognitive ergonomics extends to team collaboration and communication. Designing collaborative tools and environments that support effective information sharing, coordination, and decision-making among team members enhances overall team performance.

As technologies like virtual and augmented reality become more prevalent, cognitive ergonomics becomes critical in designing immersive experiences. Ensuring that virtual environments align with human cognitive processes enhances usability and reduces mental strain.

Cognitive ergonomics are a vital aspect of designing systems and tasks that accommodate human cognitive capabilities. By understanding how people perceive, process, and respond to information, organisations can create environments that optimise mental performance, reduce cognitive load, and enhance overall user satisfaction and effectiveness. This way stress and anxiety are reduced.

Organisational Ergonomics, also known as macro-ergonomics, is a branch of ergonomics that focuses on optimising the overall organisational structure, policies, and processes to enhance efficiency, well-being, and overall system performance. This aspect of ergonomics considers the interactions among individuals, groups, and the broader organisational context.

Organisational ergonomics involves aligning workforce planning and job design with organisational goals and employee capabilities. This includes creating roles that match the skills and competencies of employees, optimizing job rotations, and ensuring that workload is distributed appropriately.

Effective communication and collaboration are essential components of organisational ergonomics. Designing communication channels, collaborative tools, and team structures that facilitate information flow and teamwork contributes to organisational efficiency and employee satisfaction.

The role of leadership and management is a critical aspect of organisational ergonomics. Effective leaders understand and respond to the needs of their teams, create a positive work culture, and implement management practices that align with ergonomic principles.

Organisational ergonomics addresses decision-making processes within the organisation. This includes evaluating the clarity of decision-making structures, ensuring that decision authority is appropriately distributed, and promoting transparency in decision-making.

The culture of an organisation significantly influences employee behaviour, motivation, and job satisfaction. Organisational ergonomics involves shaping a positive culture that supports employee well-being, fosters innovation, and aligns with the overall goals of the organisation.

Organisational ergonomics includes the design of training and development programs that enhance employee skills, adaptability, and overall job performance. These programs contribute to the organisation's ability to adapt to changes in the business environment.

The need for designing performance management systems that are fair, transparent, and aligned with organisational goals is a key consideration in organisational ergonomics. This includes setting realistic performance expectations, providing constructive feedback, and ensuring that recognition and rewards are appropriately distributed.

Companies that prioritise the health and well-being of their employees align with organisational ergonomics principles. This involves implementing wellness programs, providing access to healthcare resources, and creating a supportive environment that promotes a healthy work-life balance.

Using this type of ergonomics, the value of how organisations manage change is studied, including the evaluation of the impact changes have on employees, the effective communication during transitions, and the provision of the necessary support to help employees adapt to new circumstances.

Organisational ergonomics encompasses various aspects of organisational design, management practices, and policies that impact the well-being and performance of employees. By aligning these elements with ergonomic principles, organisations can create a more efficient, adaptive, and supportive work environment, ultimately contributing to the overall success of the organisation.

If we analyse Biomechanical Ergonomics, we will find some similarities with previous categories, mainly Physical ergonomics. Despite this, Biomechanical ergonomics sometimes goes more in depth. It is a branch of ergonomics that focuses on understanding the mechanical aspects of the human body's movements and physical capabilities in the context of work-related activities.

The goal is to design workspaces, tools, and tasks that minimise physical strain, reduce the risk of musculoskeletal disorders, and optimise overall performance.

Biomechanical ergonomics involves a deep understanding of how the human body moves, the forces exerted on joints and muscles, and

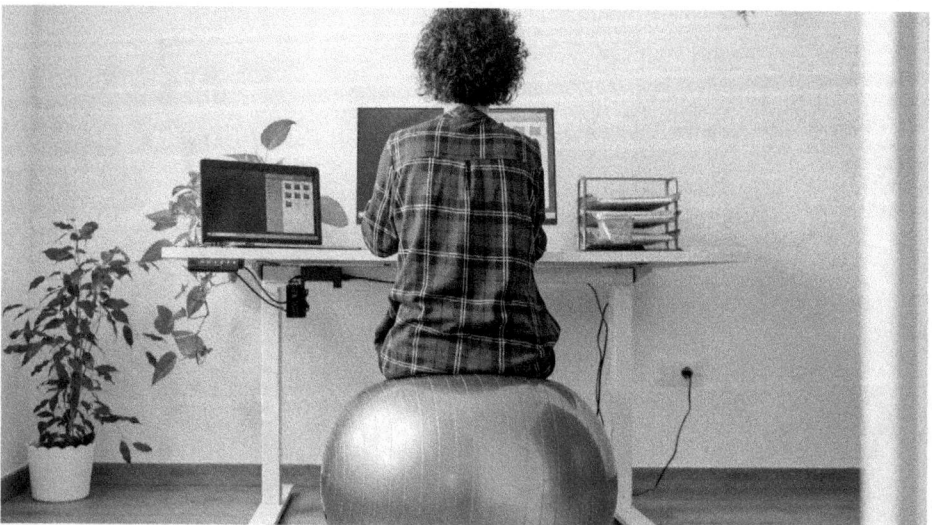

the limitations of different body parts. This knowledge is essential for designing tasks and work environments that align with the biomechanical capabilities of workers.

This is applied to the design of tasks and physical workload. It includes considering the forces required for specific tasks, the range of motion of different body parts, and the duration of physical activities. Task design aims to minimise excessive forces and repetitive movements that can lead to injuries.

One of the key applications of biomechanical ergonomics is in the design of lifting and manual handling tasks. This includes setting guidelines for safe lifting techniques, designing equipment to assist with heavy lifting, and providing training on proper body mechanics to prevent back injuries.

Designing tools and equipment with biomechanical principles in mind is crucial for reducing physical strain. This involves considering grip design, handle heights, and force requirements to ensure that workers can perform tasks without excessive force or awkward postures.

Biomechanical ergonomics addresses the design of workspaces to promote optimal posture and reduce the risk of musculoskeletal disorders.

This includes designing chairs, desks, and workstations that support a natural and comfortable alignment of the spine, limbs, and joints.

Understanding how forces are distributed across different joints and muscles during various activities is central to biomechanical ergonomics. By optimising force distribution, ergonomic designs aim to minimise the risk of overloading specific joints and tissues.

Biomechanical ergonomics addresses strategies for managing physical fatigue. This involves designing work-rest schedules, providing ergonomic seating and support, and considering factors such as muscle fatigue and recovery time during task design.

The biomechanical ergonomics approach considers the physical fitness and capabilities of workers. This includes recognising that individuals may have different strength levels, ranges of motion, and physical conditions, and designing tasks accordingly to accommodate these variations.

It emphasises the importance of training workers on proper body mechanics. Education on lifting techniques, posture awareness, and ergonomic principles contributes to injury prevention and the overall well-being of the workforce.

So, biomechanical ergonomics is essential for creating work environments that are physically supportive, minimise the risk of injuries, and optimise the efficiency of tasks. By applying biomechanical principles, organisations can enhance the physical well-being of their workforce and contribute to long-term health and safety.

Finally, Environmental ergonomics focuses on the design of the physical environment to optimise human well-being, comfort, and performance. It involves creating spaces that are conducive to work, reduce stressors, and enhance overall efficiency.

Environmental ergonomics considers the impact of temperature on individuals' comfort and performance. Designing spaces with proper heating, ventilation, and air conditioning systems ensures thermal comfort, preventing discomfort and productivity decline associated with extreme temperatures.

Lighting is a crucial aspect of environmental ergonomics. Proper lighting design, considering natural and artificial lighting sources, helps prevent eyestrain, reduces fatigue, and enhances visual comfort. It also supports the circadian rhythm (the changes of the body during the day), influencing mood and alertness.

It addresses noise control measures to create acoustically comfortable work environments. By minimising noise disruptions, workers can focus better, reduce stress, and improve overall well-being. This is particularly important in open office settings and industrial workplaces.

Ensuring good indoor air quality is a key consideration in environmental

ergonomics. Proper ventilation, control of pollutants, and access to fresh air contribute to a healthier workplace, reducing the risk of respiratory issues and enhancing overall cognitive function.

The layout and design of workspaces are essential in environmental ergonomics. Properly arranging furniture, equipment, and partitions can enhance the flow of work, facilitate collaboration, and create an efficient and aesthetically pleasing environment. This includes the impact of colour and aesthetics on mood and well-being. The choice of colours, textures, and overall aesthetics in the workplace can influence the psychological and emotional state of individuals, contributing to a positive and motivating atmosphere.

In addition ergonomic furniture design is crucial for environmental ergonomics. Chairs, desks, and other furniture should be designed to support good posture, provide comfort, and accommodate a variety of body sizes and shapes. This helps prevent musculoskeletal issues and enhances overall user satisfaction.

Environmental ergonomics considers the accessibility and inclusivity of spaces for individuals with diverse needs. Designing environments that are accessible to people with disabilities ensures that everyone can navigate and use the space comfortably.

Incorporating elements of nature, known as biophilic design, is a trend in

environmental ergonomics.

**But what is biophilic?**
Biophilic refers to the concept of bio-philia (Bio = Life or Nature and Phillia = Friendship so in free translation is the Like or Love of Nature. Such an environment you may encounter while reading this book), which is the innate human tendency to seek connections with nature and other forms of life. The term "biophilic" is often used to describe design principles, environments, or practices that incorporate natural elements, patterns, and processes to enhance well-being, productivity, and the overall experience of occupants.

Biophilic design is an approach that aims to bring nature into the built environment, recognising the positive impacts it can have on human health and happiness. Biophilic design principles can be applied in various settings, including homes, offices, schools, and public spaces. Access to natural light, indoor plants, and views of nature can positively impact mental well-being, reduce stress, and enhance overall job satisfaction. The goal of biophilic design is to create environments that support the physical, mental, and emotional well-being of individuals by fostering a deeper connection with the natural world. This approach is based on the understanding that incorporating nature into our surroundings can have positive effects on stress reduction, creativity, cognitive function, and overall satisfaction. As a result, biophilic design has gained popularity in various fields, including architecture, interior design, and urban planning.

Environmental ergonomics adapts to the growing trend of flexible work arrangements. Designing flexible workspaces that accommodate various work styles, such as hot-desking, remote work, and collaborative spaces, supports the changing needs of the workforce.

Environmental ergonomics includes considerations for safety and emergency preparedness. Well-designed emergency exits, clear signage, and easily accessible safety equipment contribute to a safe work environment.

Environmental ergonomics plays a critical role in creating work environments that promote physical and mental well-being, enhance productivity, and support the diverse needs of the workforce. By addressing factors such as temperature, lighting, noise, and overall design, organizations can create spaces that contribute to a positive and effective work experience.

It is a very common observation that these very simple guidelines are not followed, and there are managers who are even ignoring them.

But how does the lack or failure to follow this ergonomic guidance affect the business?

Such a case can have a range of negative effects, impacting both the well-being of employees and the overall performance of the organisation. The absence of ergonomic considerations can affect a business in multiple ways.

It may increase the risk of Musculoskeletal Disorders.

But what do I mean by musculoskeletal?

Musculoskeletal refers to the musculoskeletal system, which is the combination of the muscular and skeletal systems in the human body. This system is responsible for providing structure, support, and movement. The term "musculoskeletal" is often used to describe conditions, disorders, or issues related to the muscles, bones, joints, ligaments, tendons, and other connective tissues.

Some of the conditions could be:
Musculoskeletal issues/conditions can result from various factors, including age, genetics, overuse, trauma, and autoimmune disorders. Managing and preventing musculoskeletal issues often involves a combination of medical interventions, physical therapy, lifestyle modifications, and ergonomic considerations to ensure a healthy and functional musculoskeletal system.

Poor ergonomic design in workspaces, such as uncomfortable chairs, poorly designed desks, or improper computer setups, can contribute to an increased risk of musculoskeletal disorders. Employees may experience

**Tendonitis:** Inflammation of tendons, often caused by overuse or repetitive motion.

**Muscle Strains and Sprains:** Overstretching or tearing of muscles or ligaments.

**Fractures:** Breaks or cracks in bones.

**Disk Herniation:** The displacement of the soft, cushion-like discs between spinal vertebrae.

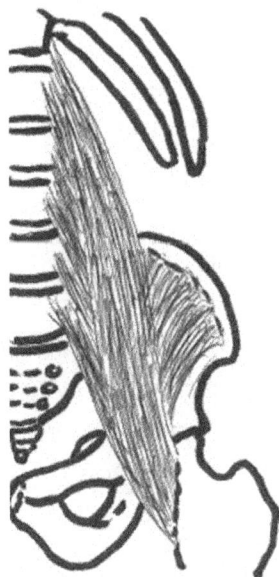

conditions like back pain, neck strain, carpal tunnel syndrome, and other physical discomforts.

Discomfort and pain resulting from inadequate ergonomic conditions can lead to decreased productivity. Employees who are physically uncomfortable or fatigued are likely to be less focused, make more errors, and have reduced work efficiency.

Unaddressed ergonomic issues may lead to increased absenteeism as employees may need to take time off to recover from injuries or seek medical treatment for work-related health problems.

Businesses may incur higher healthcare costs due to employees seeking medical attention for ergonomic-related health issues. This includes expenses related to medical treatment, rehabilitation, and potential workers' compensation claims.

Lack of consideration for ergonomic principles can contribute to lower employee engagement and satisfaction. When employees feel that their well-being is not prioritised, morale and job satisfaction may decline, leading to higher turnover rates, as employees may seek employment elsewhere in search of a more supportive and healthier work environment.

Failure to adhere to occupational health and safety regulations or address workplace conditions that contribute to health issues may result in legal challenges and regulatory penalties.

A poor reputation for workplace ergonomics can negatively impact a company's ability to attract top talent. Potential employees may consider ergonomic factors when evaluating job opportunities, and a lack of attention to these considerations can be a deterrent.

Discomfort and physical strain can hinder employees' ability to think creatively and innovatively. A workplace that prioritizes ergonomics is more likely to foster an environment where employees can perform at their best.

A lack of attention to ergonomic considerations can contribute to a negative workplace culture. Employees may perceive a lack of concern for their well-being, leading to decreased morale and a less positive work atmosphere.

The absence of ergonomics in a business can have widespread implications, affecting the health and productivity of employees, increasing operational costs, and influencing the overall success and reputation of the organization. Implementing ergonomic practices is not only a matter of compliance but also a strategic investment in the well-being and performance of the workforce.

The most common musculoskeletal problem we have when ergonomics are not followed is spinal injuries. The result is mostly either neck pain or low back pain.

What happen if objects are positioned wrongly at work? How does this affects the low back pain sufferer?

If objects in a workspace are positioned incorrectly for an individual suffering from low back pain, it can exacerbate their discomfort and potentially lead to further issues.

Here are some ways improper positioning can affect a low back pain sufferer:

1.  **Poor Posture:** Incorrectly positioned objects, such as a chair that lacks lumbar support or a desk that is too high or too low, can contribute to poor posture. Poor posture is a common factor in low back pain.

2. **Increased Strain on the Lower Back:** Improperly positioned chairs, desks, or monitors can force individuals into awkward postures, leading to increased strain on the lower back. This can contribute to muscle tension and discomfort.

3. **Muscle Fatigue:** Constantly adjusting or straining to reach objects due to poor positioning can lead to muscle fatigue in the lower back. Over time, this can contribute to chronic pain and discomfort.

4. **Repetitive Stress Injuries:** Prolonged periods of poor positioning or repetitive movements can contribute to repetitive stress injuries, including those affecting the lower back. This can lead to chronic conditions such as herniated discs or sciatica.

5. **Limited Range of Motion:** Incorrectly positioned objects may limit the individual's ability to move freely. This limitation can affect their range of motion and contribute to stiffness and pain.

6. **Increased Discomfort during Work Hours:** Spending long hours in an ergonomically unfriendly environment can increase discomfort and pain levels for someone with low back pain. This may negatively impact their ability to focus and perform tasks efficiently.

Ergonomics play a crucial role in preventing and managing low back pain. If objects such as chairs, desks, or keyboards are not set up according to ergonomic principles, it can contribute to discomfort and exacerbate existing issues.

To address these issues, it's important to ensure that the workspace is properly set up with ergonomic principles in mind. This includes adjusting the height of the chair and desk, positioning the monitor at eye level, and using ergonomic accessories like lumbar supports or footrests. Regular breaks and movement throughout the day can also help reduce the impact of prolonged sitting. Individuals with persistent low back pain should seek advice from healthcare professionals for personalised recommendations.

Managers who underwent the Professional Prime Pathway method learned how to implement the M.I.R. system. As it is obvious, there is another acronym here, and this correspond to the Management of employees who are Low Back Pain Sufferers, to the organisation of the correct installation of the different objects around their work force, and by following the simple ergonomic guidelines, how to reduce the injuries within the company.

Management of Ergonomics however, has two entities. The first is to know how to manage ergonomics, and the second is how to manage ergonomics in conjunction with low back pain suffering employees.

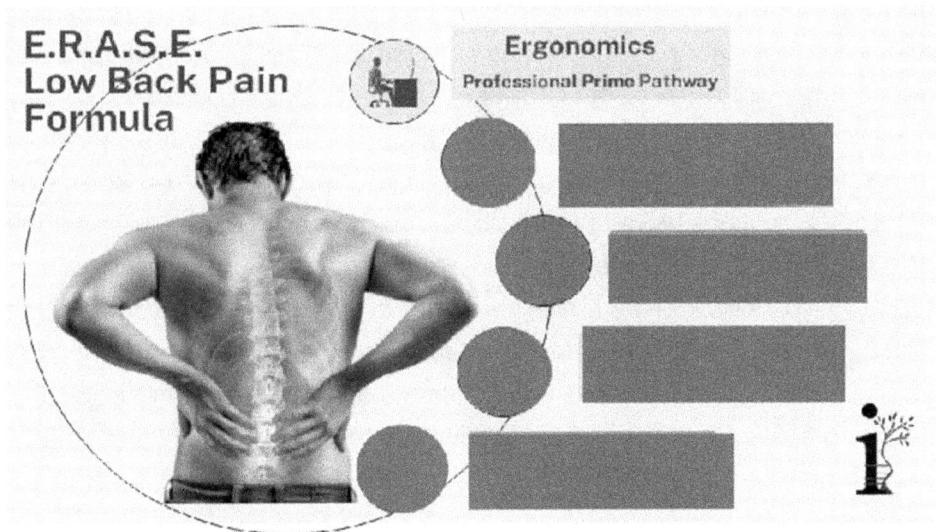

**E.R.A.S.E.**
**Low Back Pain**
**Formula**

Ergonomics
Professional Prime Pathway

To manage ergonomics, the manager has to define ergonomics and its significance in the workplace. They need to understand that effective management of ergonomics contributes to employee well-being, productivity, and overall organisational success. They have to emphasise the role of ergonomics in preventing work-related injuries and promoting employee health. They need to describe the benefits of ergonomics by pointing out how such a discipline can improve productivity by leading to increased efficiency and reduced absenteeism. Proper implementation of ergonomics can minimise health-related absenteeism and improve employee satisfaction, as a comfortable work environment is linked with job satisfaction.

An ergonomic assessment and planning has to be mapped out by explaining the process of conducting an ergonomics assessment in the workplace. Risk factors and potential areas for improvement have to be identified. The importance of involving employees in the planning process to address individual needs has to be emphasised. Special necessary equipment has to be discussed following the assessment, and the design of workspaces can impact posture and comfort. The possibility of the importance of providing adjustable equipment to accommodate different body types and preferences has to be highlighted. A continuous training and education programme has to be established as the significance of educating employees about proper ergonomics has to be stressed. They have to be trained and be aware of the correct posture, the necessity of breaks, and their overall well-being. Both the board of the company and the employees have to learn about the advances of new technology and work practices as these evolve constantly. In the whole scheme of ergonomics management, the necessity of integration with the Health and Safety Programme would be beneficial, as the ways that ergonomics fits into broader health and safety initiatives will be emphasised, and new strategies for injury prevention will be explored. Finally, the role of ergonomics and the link with Health and Safety regulations need to be highlighted.

Understanding the importance of managing ergonomics for the well-being of employees and the success of the organisation is paramount, and a continuous improvement and adaptation to changing work environments and technologies hasve to be encouraged.

Managing ergonomics in conjunction with back pain on the other hand involves a targeted approach to create a work environment that not only adheres to ergonomic principles but also addresses and mitigates the specific challenges associated with back pain. It will be necessary to arrange:

1. **Individualized Assessments:** Health Screenings by conducting health assessments or surveys to identify employees experiencing back pain. Individual consultations by offering one-on-one ergonomic consultation to employees with back pain and trying to understand their specific needs may be very helpful.

2. **Customised Ergonomic Solutions:** Adaptive Furniture by providing ergonomic furniture that can be customised to support employees

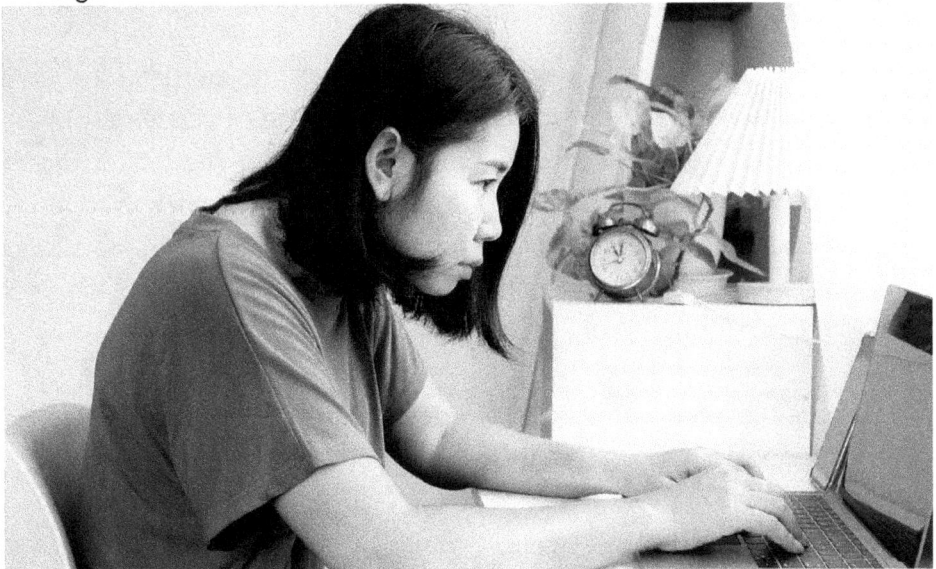

with back pain, such as chairs with adjustable lumbar support. Sit-Stand Desks can be implemented as they can offer a sit-stand position because they allow employees to change their working position throughout the day, which can be particularly beneficial for those with back pain.

3. **Training Programs:** Back Health Education by developing training programs that focus on educating employees about maintaining a healthy back, proper lifting techniques, and exercises to alleviate back pain or even Posture Workshops where people will learn how to maintain their proper posture while sitting and standing to reduce strain on the back.

4. **Accommodations for Medical Conditions:** Flexible Work Arrangements as people may need flexibility at work due to their chronic back pain problems. Part-time telecommuting or modified work hours for example would be useful arrangement to those who are suffering. A Job Modification may be considered for employees with severe back pain, such as adjusting tasks or providing assistive devices.

5. **Physical Therapy Services:** On-Site Services can be provided only if it is feasible, an offer that can easily help the physical as well as the mental wellbeing of the employees. Similarly, such provision can be arranged with nearby facilities for employees with back pain. Such service can help the management as a quick, clear, and trusty feedback on the employee's condition that can provide vital information for the future prognosis.

Exercise Programmes can be promoted at workplace by focusing on strengthening the core muscles to support the back.

6. **Workspace Modification:** Supply ergonomic accessories such as lumbar support cushions, footrests, or anti-fatigue mats can enhance the comfort and reduce strain on the back. Different equipment sush as computer monitors needs to be at eye level to prevent employees from hunching over or straining their necks.

7. **Regular Check-ins:** Frequent Health and Safety Meetings need to be organised and the condition and issues that may rise from the back have to be analysed and solved. These meetings have to be scheduled by the health and safety personnel and the employees who have reported back pain need to be assessed and the effectiveness of any interventions has to be monitored. Necessary adjustments of any equipment have to be followed up for their correctness and potential further alterations could be made if needed.

8. **Pain Management Resources:** Provide information on pain management resources, such as access to healthcare professionals, pain clinics, or employee assistance programs or even support groups. There are companies who establish support groups or forums where employees can share experiences and coping strategies for managing back pain.

9. **Wellness Programs:** Incorporate overall wellness initiatives that include stress reduction and mental health support, as psychological factors can contribute to back pain. Introduce mind-body practices like yoga or meditation that can help alleviate stress and promote back health.

10. **Documentation and Compliance:** Keep detailed records of ergonomic assessments, interventions, and employee feedback to demonstrate compliance with health and safety regulations. Stay informed about relevant laws and regulations regarding accommodations for employees with disabilities, including back pain.

By integrating back pain management into the broader ergonomics strategy, organisations can create a more inclusive and supportive workplace that considers the unique needs of employees dealing with back pain. Regular communication and a proactive approach to addressing issues are critical for success.

Here is the story of Michael, a manager in a software company who was a results-oriented leader. He was pushing his team to meet deadlines and exceed expectations. When he found that there were employees who were experiencing low back pain, Michael became concerned. He was worried that due to their pain, productivity would be influenced and that deadlines would not be met. His initial approach was worry, anxiety, and frustration, as he focused solely on the lost time and the failure to meet their targets. He forgot that he was managing human beings and he was fixated on the products and the impact on the company's performance.

Following our discussions, Michael found time to participate in meetings and learn that many of his employees were experiencing pain and discomfort due to poor posture they were forced to have in their workstations, as there was not consideration given to ergonomics at all. Following this experience and the new information, he decided to implement ergonomics as a solution to help his employees manage their low back pain.

The result of his efforts brought transformation within his company. People became more productive, developed a sense of comfort, and the entire workforce was happy with the attention received. Michael was their hero, as he understood their needs.

Michael realised the importance of ergonomics in promoting employee well-being. By implementing ergonomic design principles in the workplace, he was able to reduce strain and discomfort, allowing his employees to work more comfortably and effectively.

He learned, with the help of experts, the importance of assessing every suffering employee and he overlooked the development of custom -made equipment for every individual according to their specifications in ergonomic design. By providing adjustable workstations and chairs, he allowed his employees to tailor their work environment to their individual needs, promoting comfort and productivity.

He developed training to promote ergonomic awareness. By providing his employees with training on proper ergonomic practices and the importance of posture, he empowered them to take control of their own health and well-being.

He established a continuous assessment programme and the need for updating the ergonomic design of the workplace. This way, he ensured that his employees' needs were always being met, promoting long-term health and productivity.

Following an understanding of management, people have to learn about the correct linstallation of different objects around their employees. But how should objects be installed according to ergonomics for an individual suffering from low back pain?

For individuals experiencing low back pain, setting up an ergonomic workspace is crucial to alleviate discomfort and promote a healthier posture. But how is it possible? What will be needed?

Initially, an ergonomic chair may be necessary. The choice of a chair with good lumbar support would be beneficial. This helps maintain the natural curve of the spine and reduces stress on the lower back. The chair's height has to be adjustable so that the feet are flat on the floor, and the knees are at a 90-degree angle.

The desk height has to be correct.  When sitting, the elbows should be at a 90-degree angle when resting on the desk. If possible, a sit-stand desk could be used to allow for changes in posture throughout the day.

The position of the monitor has to be at eye level to reduce strain on the neck and upper back and has to be kept at about an arm's length away. It may be necessary to use an ergonomic keyboard and mouse to reduce strain on the hands and wrists. The keyboard and mouse have to be kept close enough to avoid reaching.

In case the feet don't comfortably touch the floor, the use of a footrest could be considered. This helps in maintain proper leg and lower back alignment.

It will be necessary to take regular breaks to stand, stretch, and move around. Prolonged sitting can contribute to back pain. Gentle stretching exercises specifically targeting the lower back should be incorporated into the routine.

The correct posture while sitting is the one that facilitates the person to sit back in their chair, keeping their back straight and shoulders relaxed. They have to avoid slouching or leaning forward for extended periods.

If a laptop is used, an external keyboard and mouse can be considered to avoid awkward postures. A laptop stand helping to bring the screen to eye level will be very beneficial.

Proper lighting to reduce eye strain has to be provided. The desk has to be positioned in such a way so that natural light doesn't cause glare on the monitor.

In case of the need for extra support, a cushion or lumbar roll can be used.

It's essential to consult with a healthcare professional for personalised advice based on your specific condition. They can provide tailored recommendations and exercises to help manage and prevent low back pain. Additionally, listen to your body, and if you experience persistent discomfort, consider seeking medical advice.

Ergonomics reduce the risk of injury, particularly back pain injuries. Reducing the risk of back pain through ergonomic practices involves implementing proper workplace design and habits that promote a healthier posture and minimize strain on the back. Research and studies consistently provide evidence supporting the relationship between ergonomics and injury reduction in the workplace.

Numerous studies have demonstrated the effectiveness of ergonomic interventions in reducing the risk of musculoskeletal disorders (MSDs). For example, a systematic review published in the journal "Applied Ergonomics" (2017) found that ergonomic interventions in the workplace were associated with a significant reduction in the prevalence of injuries, particularly in the neck, shoulders, and upper extremities.

Proper ergonomic design of workstations, chairs, and equipment has been shown to improve posture and increase comfort, reducing the likelihood of injuries. A study published in the "Journal of Occupational Rehabilitation" (2019) found that the use of an ergonomic chair significantly improved sitting posture and reduced discomfort in office workers.

Ergonomic interventions aimed at minimising repetitive motions and awkward postures can contribute to a decreased risk of repetitive strain injuries. Research published in the "Journal of Occupational and Environmental Medicine" (2017) indicated that ergonomic modifications in a poultry processing plant led to a significant reduction in the incidence among workers.

Lower back pain is a common issue in the workplace, and ergonomics plays a crucial role in addressing and preventing it. A study published in the "Journal of Occupational and Environmental Medicine" (2018) found that ergonomic interventions, such as adjustable chairs and workstation modifications, were effective in reducing lower back pain among office workers.

In healthcare settings, where manual patient handling tasks are common, ergonomic interventions have shown to be effective in reducing injuries. A study published in the "American Journal of Industrial Medicine" (2017) reported that implementing ergonomic interventions, including training and the use of lifting devices, resulted in a significant reduction in musculoskeletal injuries among healthcare workers.

Beyond the direct health benefits, there is evidence supporting the economic advantages of ergonomics in injury reduction. A study published in the "Journal of Safety Research" (2017) found that investments in ergonomic interventions resulted in substantial cost savings due to

reduced workers' compensation claims and healthcare expenses.

Research has also demonstrated the long-term impact of ergonomic interventions on injury reduction. A longitudinal study published in the "American Journal of Industrial Medicine" (2018) found that sustained ergonomic interventions led to a significant decrease in the incidence of work-related musculoskeletal injuries over several years.

These findings collectively provide strong evidence supporting the effectiveness of ergonomics in reducing workplace injuries. Implementing ergonomic principles in the design of workspaces, tools, and tasks can lead to improved employee health, increased productivity, and significant cost savings for businesses.

Below you may find some sites to research further information:

- **Occupational Safety and Health Administration (OSHA)**
  - OSHA - Computer Workstations eTool

- **Mayo Clinic - Computer Workstation Ergonomics**
  - Mayo Clinic - Office Ergonomics: Your How-To Guide

- **Canadian Centre for Occupational Health and Safety (CCOHS)**
  - CCOHS - Ergonomics in the Office

- **National Institute for Occupational Safety and Health (NIOSH)**
  - NIOSH - Ergonomics and Musculoskeletal Disorders

- **American Academy of Orthopaedic Surgeons (AAOS)**
  - AAOS - Office Ergonomics

- **Back Care - The Charity for Back and Neck Pain**

- ° Back Care - Work and Ergonomics

- **Centers for Disease Control and Prevention (CDC)**

- **American Optometric Association (AOA)**

Following extensive exploration of the factors of management, installation, and reduction and their impact on back pain within the workplace, a compelling narrative emerges — one that underscores the pivotal role of strategic approaches in mitigating the challenges associated with back pain. As we conclude this analysis, it is evident that effective management practices, thoughtful installation of ergonomic solutions, and a commitment to reducing risk factors collectively contribute to a workplace environment that not only addresses back pain but also fosters a culture of well-being and productivity.

Management practices play a central role in creating a work environment that supports back health. From implementing ergonomic policies to fostering a culture of open communication, effective management is instrumental in preventing and addressing back pain issues. Proactive management approaches recognise the significance of employee health, contributing to a workplace culture that prioritizes both physical and mental well-being.

The installation of ergonomic solutions, ranging from adjustable furniture to optimised workspace layouts, emerges as a crucial factor in our exploration. Thoughtful installation contributes to sustainable comfort by promoting proper posture, reducing strain, and creating workspaces that align with ergonomic principles. This not only prevents back pain but also enhances overall comfort and productivity for employees.

The concept of reduction underscores the importance of minimising risk factors associated with back pain. This involves identifying and addressing elements such as prolonged sitting, poor posture, and inadequate support. Through reduction strategies, workplaces can create an environment that actively mitigates potential causes of back pain, leading to a healthier and more resilient workforce.

The integration of effective management practices, ergonomic installation, and strategic reduction efforts into the workplace yields a multitude of benefits. Reduced instances of back pain, increased employee satisfaction, heightened productivity, and a positive organisational culture are among the outcomes. By recognising the impact of these factors on back health, workplaces can create an environment that not only prevents and manages back pain but also nurtures the physical, mental, and emotional well-being of their employees.

Finally, our exploration advocates for a proactive and strategic approach to back health in the workplace. By embracing effective management, thoughtful installation of ergonomic solutions, and a commitment to reducing risk factors, organisations can pave the way for a future where individuals not only thrive professionally but also experience a profound sense of well-being. The benefits extend far beyond the workplace, shaping a society where holistic health is championed, and individuals are empowered to lead fulfilling and resilient lives.

Going back to Michael's experience, he felt a deep sense of concern and responsibility towards his employees. He recognised that their pain not only affected their ability to work effectively but also posed a risk of long-term injury. He worried about the impact on employee morale and the company's performance.

He realised that his initial approach of asking them only about their symptoms and concentrating on productivity was not yielding positive results, so he decided to prioritise the well-being of his employees by implementing correct ergonomic management and installation. He educated himself on the principles of ergonomics and consulted with experts to identify the most effective solutions for his team. With their guidance, he oversaw the installation of ergonomic equipment throughout the company, including adjustable desks, ergonomic chairs, and proper lighting. These changes were aimed at reducing the risk of injuries and promoting better posture and comfort among employees.

As a result of his efforts, he witnessed a significant improvement in employee well-being and a reduction in injuries within the company. Morale improved, and productivity soared as employees felt more comfortable and supported in their work environment. He felt a sense of pride and satisfaction knowing that he had made a positive impact on his team's health and safety.

The main lessons he had learned were that the well-being of his employees should always be a top priority. By investing in ergonomic management and installation, he demonstrated his commitment to creating a safe and supportive work environment.

The next part that was necessary was education. It was very important to educate himself on the principles of ergonomics. By understanding the factors contributing to low back pain and discomfort, he was better equipped to address the issue effectively.

For this latter, he engaged with experts who could guide him in the implementation of the different ergonomic solutions. By consulting these professionals in the field, he was able to identify the most effective strategies for reducing injuries and promoting employee wellness.

The best lesson he learned, though, was the importance of involving employees in the decision-making process. By soliciting their input and feedback, he ensured that the ergonomic solutions implemented were tailored to their needs and preferences.

With their agreement, he created a safe and ergonomic work environment as an ongoing process. He committed to regularly monitoring and adjusting the ergonomic measures in place to ensure they remained effective and relevant as the company grew and evolved.

In the end, his journey taught him valuable lessons about the importance of prioritising employee well-being, educating himself on ergonomic principles, consulting with experts, involving employees in decision-making, and continuously monitoring and adjusting ergonomic measures. By implementing correct ergonomic management and installation, he was able to significantly reduce injuries and promote a safer, more comfortable work environment for his employees, leading to positive outcomes for both the employees and the company as a whole.

# 2

## CHAPTER

## RANGE

## What do I mean by RANGE?

Every being has a certain range of movement of its body as a whole or in each different joint. Additionally, different beings have different ranges of motion when comparing the same joints. The same applies to human beings. Among all humans, the ranges of the joints differ, even when comparing the same joint. This difference may result from ligament laxity, muscle strength, or potential joint pathology within the joint itself.

Range of motion refers to the extent of movement that a joint can go through in various directions. It is a measurement that describes the flexibility and mobility of a specific joint in the body. Range of motion is typically assessed in terms of degrees of movement and can be influenced by various factors, including the structure of the joint, surrounding muscles, tendons, ligaments, and the overall health of the individual.

Assessing and maintaining an optimal range of motion in the joints is essential for overall mobility, flexibility, and functionality. Factors that can affect range of motion include age, gender, genetics, physical activity level, and any existing injuries or medical conditions. Physical therapists often use range of motion assessments to evaluate joint health and develop targeted exercise programs to improve or maintain flexibility and prevent joint-related issues. Maintaining a healthy range of motion is crucial for performing daily activities, sports, and preventing musculoskeletal problems.

The range of motion in the context of the spine refers to the extent to which a person can flex, extend, rotate, and laterally bend their lower back. Limited range of motion can be associated with low back pain, and the relationship between the two is often complex. But what are the potential limiting factors when examining spinal movements, and how can they be improved?

Limitation of range of motion in the lower back can be caused by muscle imbalances and stiffness. When certain muscles are tight and others are weak, it can restrict the movement of the spine. This imbalance may contribute to poor posture and increased stress on the lower back, leading to pain. Tight hamstrings, hip flexors, and lower back muscles can limit the ability to bend forward or rotate the spine, potentially causing discomfort or pain.

A restricted range of motion in the lower back can affect daily activities, including bending, lifting, and twisting. Individuals with limited flexibility may adopt compensatory movements, putting additional strain on the lower back and increasing the risk of injury or pain.

Conditions such as degenerative disc disease or osteoarthritis can contribute to a reduction in the range of motion in the lower back. These conditions may lead to stiffness, pain, and a gradual loss of flexibility over time.

Maintaining proper spinal alignment is essential for a healthy range of motion. Poor alignment, such as excessive curvature (lordosis) or flattening of the spine, can contribute to musculoskeletal imbalances and increase the risk of low back pain.

On the other hand, ergonomics plays a role in maintaining a healthy range of motion and preventing low back pain. Proper ergonomic design of workstations, chairs, and equipment can help individuals maintain good posture and reduce the risk of developing musculoskeletal issues, including low back pain. Regular physical activity and targeted stretching exercises can improve flexibility and range of motion in the lower back. Incorporating exercises that focus on strengthening core muscles and promoting spinal flexibility can be beneficial for preventing or alleviating low back pain.

Physical therapy is often recommended for individuals with low back pain and limited range of motion. Physical therapists can prescribe exercises and stretches tailored to improving flexibility, strengthening supporting muscles, and addressing specific issues contributing to pain.

Except for limited range of motion, other factors that may contribute to pain include poor posture, muscle weakness, and underlying medical conditions.

Individuals experiencing persistent or severe low back pain should seek professional medical advice for a comprehensive assessment and appropriate management strategies.

In some cases, people in high positions in the industry  may force their employees to exceed the limitations of the range of motion the joint is able to perform. In cases like those, an injury may be the result and that can lead to absences, sick leaves, and potentially complaints and litigation. Is this something a company has to have? Can business leaders afford these expenses?

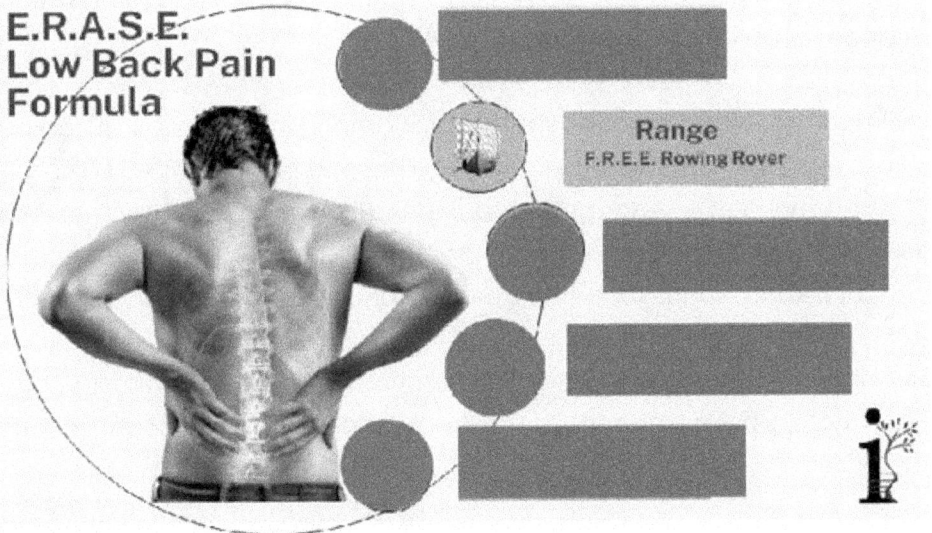

E.R.A.S.E.
Low Back Pain
Formula

Range
F.R.E.E. Rowing Rover

People who followed the F.R.E.E. Rowing Rover learned the importance of body flexibility, the resilience a person with low back pain must have to continue thriving within their work, the efficiency of body function, the mechanics of the spine, and finally, the endocrine part of the body and how various hormones could help with pain management.

Flexibility refers to the ability of a joint or a group of joints to move through a full range of motion without pain or stiffness. It is a key component of physical fitness and is influenced by factors such as muscle elasticity, joint structure, and the surrounding connective tissues.

Flexibility is not only important for athletes and dancers but also for individuals in their daily activities. Having good flexibility allows for better movement efficiency, reduces the risk of injury, and improves overall physical performance.

Flexibility can be improved through regular stretching exercises and activities that promote mobility and range of motion. There are different types of flexibility, including static flexibility (the ability to hold a stretched position), dynamic flexibility (the ability to move a joint through its full range of motion), and passive flexibility (the ability to be moved through a range of motion by an external force).

It's important to note that flexibility varies among individuals and can be influenced by factors such as age, genetics, and physical conditioning. It is recommended to engage in a balanced fitness routine that includes flexibility training along with other components such as strength, cardiovascular endurance, and balance for overall physical well-being.

Flexibility is an important factor in the context of low back pain, and can have both positive and negative implications depending on various factors.

Muscle imbalances can contribute to limited flexibility and can be related to low back pain. These could be the result of either tight muscle groups (limited flexibility in certain muscle groups, such as the hamstrings, hip flexors, and iliopsoas, can contribute to low back pain. Tight muscles may alter the biomechanics of the spine and pelvis, leading to increased stress on the lower back), or weak muscles (excessive flexibility without sufficient strength, especially in the core muscles, can lead to instability in the spine, potentially contributing to low back pain).

The mobility of the spine plays a key role in the absorption of energy. Adequate mobility in the thoracic spine can help distribute movement throughout the spine, reducing the load on the lumbar spine. However, excessive flexibility or hypermobility in the lumbar spine can contribute to instability and potentially lead to pain.

Imbalances in the pelvis area, such as anterior or posterior pelvic tilt, can affect the natural curvature of the spine and contribute to low back pain.

On top of that, poor posture, often associated with reduced flexibility, can result in increased pressure on the lumbar spine and contribute to pain.

Exercises play a crucial role in keeping the spine mobile. Gentle stretching can help alleviate muscle tightness and improve flexibility. Stretching exercises that target key muscle groups, including the hamstrings, hip flexors, and lower back, may be beneficial. But while flexibility is crucial, it should be complemented by core-strengthening exercises to provide stability and support for the spine.

Flexibility, as well as strengthening of muscles, is clear that may vary among individuals. Some people may benefit from increased flexibility, while others may need to focus more on stability. Personalised assessments by healthcare professionals or physical therapists can help determine the specific needs of an individual.

Emotional stress and tension can contribute to muscle tightness and impact flexibility. Mind-body practices, such as yoga or mindfulness, may help address both the physical and emotional aspects related to low back pain. While improving flexibility is important, it's crucial to avoid overstretching or engaging in activities that may exacerbate existing issues. A balanced approach that includes both flexibility and strength training is often recommended.

In conclusion, flexibility plays an important role in low back pain. Striking a balance between flexibility and strength, addressing muscle imbalances, and adopting a personalised approach are key factors in managing and preventing low back pain. Individuals experiencing persistent or severe low back pain should seek professional guidance for a comprehensive assessment and tailored recommendations.

Let's analyse now the next step, Resilience.

But what is it anyway?

Resilience refers to the ability to bounce back from adversity, adapt to challenges, and recover from difficult situations. It is the capacity to withstand and recover from stress, trauma, or setbacks and to maintain mental and emotional well-being.

There is a common quote that says, "the fall does not make you weaker but stronger, as this is a lesson and not a failure"." This is the way people

understand resilience.

Resilience is not a fixed trait but rather a skill that can be developed and strengthened over time. It involves having a positive mindset, being able to regulate emotions, having effective problem-solving skills, and having a supportive network of relationships.

Resilient individuals are able to cope with and navigate through difficult circumstances by utilizing their inner strengths and external resources. They are able to maintain a sense of purpose, optimism, and hope even in the face of adversity. Resilience is not about avoiding or denying pain, but rather about facing it, learning from it, and growing stronger as a result.

Building resilience involves developing healthy coping strategies, such as seeking support from others, maintaining a positive outlook, practicing self-care, setting realistic goals, and cultivating a sense of gratitude. It is also important to develop skills in stress management, problem-solving, and effective communication.

It is beneficial in all aspects of life, including personal relationships, work, and overall well-being. It helps individuals adapt to change, bounce back from setbacks, and thrive in the face of challenges. Developing resilience is a lifelong process that can lead to increased happiness, fulfilment, and success.

Also, it plays an important role in managing and coping with back pain. Chronic back pain can be physically and emotionally challenging and developing resilience can help individuals better navigate through the difficulties associated with it.

But how does resilience relate to back pain?

Resilience involves developing effective coping strategies to deal with pain. Resilient people are better at managing and tolerating pain, as well as finding ways to minimise its impact on their daily lives. They may engage in activities such as relaxation techniques, exercise, or mindfulness practices to help alleviate pain and improve their overall well-being.

Back pain can limit a person's physical abilities and daily activities. Resilience helps individuals adapt to these limitations by finding alternative ways to perform tasks, modifying their lifestyle, and seeking support from healthcare professionals, such as physical therapists or pain management specialists. They are more likely to explore different treatment options and make necessary lifestyle changes to improve their quality of life.

Chronic pain can have a significant impact on a person's mental and emotional well-being. Resilience involves maintaining a positive mindset and managing emotions effectively. These individuals are better equipped to cope with the emotional challenges associated with back pain, such as frustration, sadness, or anxiety. They may seek support from loved ones, join support groups, or engage in activities that promote emotional well-being, such as therapy or practicing self-care.

It can also influence an individual's commitment to treatment and rehabilitation. It takes resilience to continue with treatment plans, follow through on exercises or physical therapy sessions, and maintain a proactive approach to managing back pain. Resilient individuals are more likely to persist in their treatment, leading to better outcomes and improved overall function.

Overall, resilience in relation to back pain involves developing effective coping strategies, adapting to limitations, maintaining emotional well-being, and persisting in treatment. By cultivating resilience, people can better manage back pain, improve their quality of life, and enhance their overall well-being.

Resilient back pain sufferers may engage in a variety of activities to help alleviate their symptoms.

They can be involved in regular physical activity, which is essential for maintaining back health. These individuals may engage in exercises that strengthen the core muscles, such as Yoga, Pilates, or low impact aerobic exercises. These activities help improve posture, flexibility, and muscle strength, which can alleviate back pain and prevent future episodes.

Stretching exercises can help reduce muscle tension and improve flexibility, which can alleviate back pain. They may incorporate stretching routines into their daily routine, focusing on stretches that target the back muscles, hamstrings, and hip flexors.

Also, they may find relief from back pain through mind-body practices such as mindfulness meditation, deep breathing exercises, or progressive muscle relaxation. These practices promote relaxation, reduce stress, and help manage pain perception.

The application of heat or cold to the affected area can provide temporary relief from back pain. They may use heating pads, warm showers, or hot packs to relax muscles and increase blood flow.

Cold therapy, such as ice packs or cold compresses, can help reduce inflammation and numb the area.

They may pay attention to their posture and make adjustments to minimise strain on the back. They may use ergonomic chairs, supportive cushions, or standing desks to maintain proper alignment and reduce the risk of back pain.

Maintaining a healthy weight is important for reducing the strain on the back. Resilient individuals may engage in activities that promote weight management, such as regular exercise and a balanced diet. This can help alleviate pressure on the spine and reduce the risk of back pain.

On top of that, they are proactive in seeking professional help when needed. They may consult with healthcare professionals, such as physical therapists, chiropractors, or pain management specialists, who can provide targeted treatments, exercises, or therapies to alleviate back pain.

It's important to note that these activities should be tailored to an individual's specific condition and should be done under the guidance of a healthcare professional. What works for one person may vary for another, so it's essential to find the right combination of activities that work best for managing individual back pain.

Stretching and flexibility exercises can help reduce back pain in several ways.

Tight muscles in the back, hips, and legs can contribute to back pain. Stretching exercises target these muscles, helping to release tension and promote relaxation. By stretching regularly, they can alleviate muscle tightness and reduce the strain on the back, leading to pain relief.

Lack of flexibility in the muscles and joints can make movements more difficult and increase the risk of back pain. Stretching exercises improve flexibility by increasing the range of motion in the joints and lengthening the muscles. This increased flexibility allows for better posture, proper alignment, and improved movement patterns, reducing the likelihood of back pain.

Poor posture and spinal misalignment can put excessive stress on the back and lead to pain. Stretching exercises, particularly those that target the muscles supporting the spine, can help improve spinal alignment. By elongating and strengthening these muscles, resilient individuals can maintain a more neutral spine, reducing the strain on the back and minimizing pain.

Exercises in general increase blood flow to the muscles, including those in the back. Improved blood circulation delivers more oxygen and nutrients to the muscles, promoting their health and reducing the risk of muscle imbalances and pain. Additionally, increased blood flow helps remove waste products and toxins from the muscles, further aiding in pain relief.

Chronic stress and tension can contribute to back pain or exacerbate existing pain. Exercises promote relaxation by activating the body's relaxation response. They help release endorphins, which are natural pain-relieving and mood-enhancing chemicals. By incorporating regular stretching into their routine, resilient individuals can reduce stress levels and manage pain more effectively.

It's important to note that when engaging in stretching exercises for back pain relief, it's crucial to do so gently and gradually. Overstretching or performing stretches incorrectly can worsen the pain or cause injury. It's advisable to consult with a healthcare professional or a qualified fitness instructor to learn proper stretching techniques and to ensure that the exercises are suitable for individual needs and conditions. The next part of studying is efficiency.

Efficiency is a part of our existence. All parts of our body work in a nice and efficient way. But what is efficiency?

In scientific terms, it is a ratio between the energy spent to perform a task and the achieved result. All the organs try to work in the most efficient way, spend the minimum energy to achieve the best result. This is true. But in this piece of work, we are examining spinal efficiency as it is part of the low back pain problem.

In this part, we need to learn about the effective way the body, and mainly the spine, works.

The spine, and mainly the neural system (central nerves and brain), are the first structures that are created in our embryonic life. Fully developed, the spine is made up of a series of "cylindrical" type bones called vertebrae, together like a bicycle chain. Behind these cylindrical bones, there are arches that are linked one over the other, creating a tube, - the spinal canal. Within this canal, for most of the spine's length, runs the spinal cord, which is nerve tissue and a continuation of our brain. At the lower levels of this spinal tube, and at the end of the cord, we only have nerve roots inside the canal. Due to their appearance, we call them cauda equina, which in Latin means horse tail; this is how they look like. Along the spinal cord, we have nerve roots that come out of the canal at every level and as soon as they come out, they connect with each other at different levels, creating the peripheral nerves that run throughout the body.

The spine, if viewed from the front, is straight for its entire length, However, when viewed from the side, it is curved. There are four different curvatures, two curving forward and two curving backward. The neck and lower back

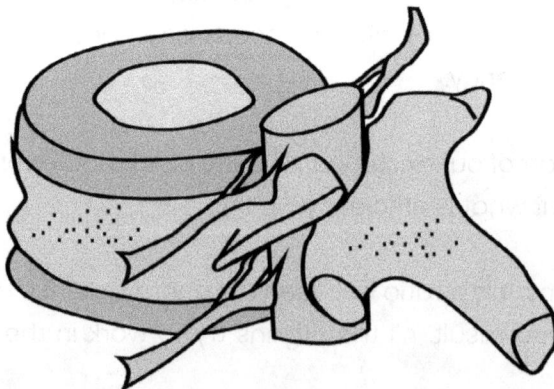

lean backwards, while the dorsal and sacral area lean forward. The forward curves are called kyphotic, and the backward curves are called lordotic. These names may help you to understand the terminology if you read a report from an investigation you have conducted. You may wonder why we need these curvatures. Imagine your spine without any curves, like a straight column. A weight is applied at the top of this column, causing a certain load. The exact magnitude of this load is transferred down to the bottom of the spine. Now let's consider a spine with curvatures. The same load is applied at the top of the column, but now the curved parts deform and absorb some of the energy, resulting in lower energy and lower load transferred directly to the bottom of the spine.

The vertebrae are linked between them with joints, which are part of the arch, called facet joints and ligaments that run in front back as well as the sides of the vertebrae. The joints are covered by their capsule and their own ligaments.

Between the vertebrae, in each level we have another fixture, the intervertebral disc. Discs are made mainly from two parts. An elastic but firm ring, called annulus and a central jelly type substance, called nucleus. The latter is under tension within the whole structure.

At the diagrams above it is evident how the nucleus that is under tension is reacting when it loaded.

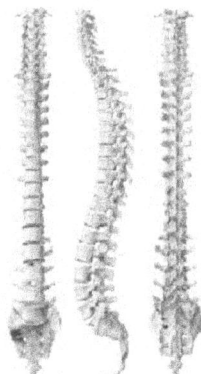

If we examine the mechanical properties of the disc we will discover, in its simplicity, that it is nothing more than a shock absorber.

Annulus is made from layers and layers of rings more or less similar structure as an onion.

The only difference between the two, aside from the shape and the smell, is the direction of the fibres in each layers. In the onion, the fibres of each layer are parallel, running from the root to the stem, and this pattern is observed in all layers.

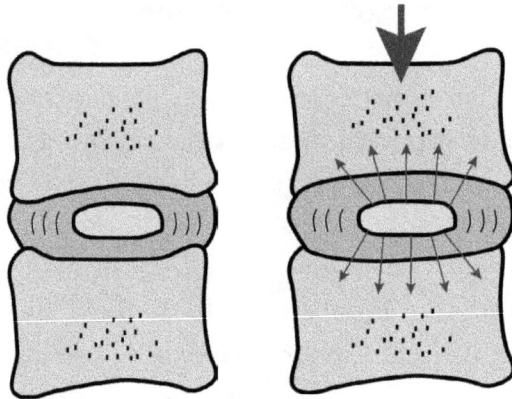

In the disc, the fibres of each layer are parallel in each layer, like the onion, but the direction differs between neighbouring layers. If one layer has an oblique direction from right to left, the one next to it will have a direction

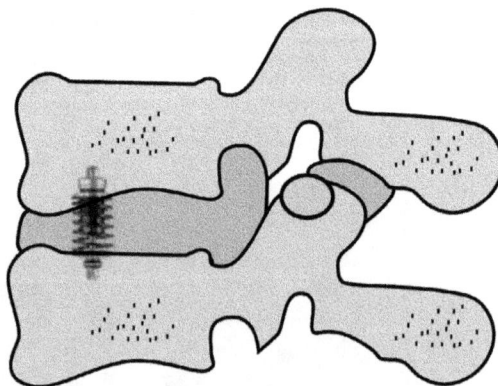

from north to south (north being the head, south being the feet), and the third layer will be oblique from left to right, and so on. This way, the sum of all layers creates a strong net, and this strength is maintained even if the body is rotated.

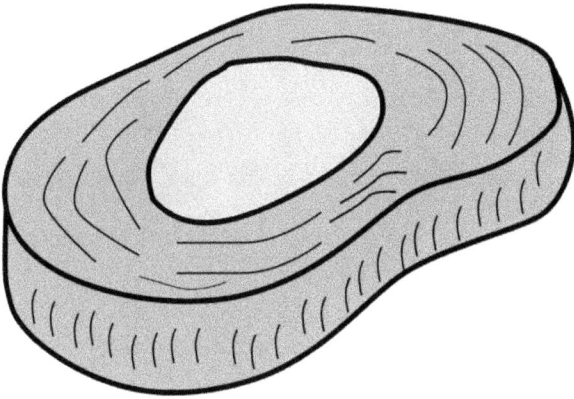

This is because the different layers rotate accordingly. For example, the layer that was running from north to south in a rotation may run obliquely from right to left, and the neighbouring layers changes accordingly. This gives the same strength to the annulus in all potential positions the body takes and protects the nucleus in the same position and with the same properties.

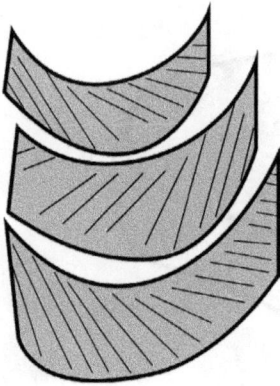

Unfortunately, as time goes by and with use, or to put it better, misuse of the spine, the entire disc structure can become "dehydrated"." In this case, the "selfish" nucleus "sucks" fluid from the neighbouring annulus in an attempt to keep its shock absorption properties. As a result, the annulus becomes "drier" and more "fragile"."

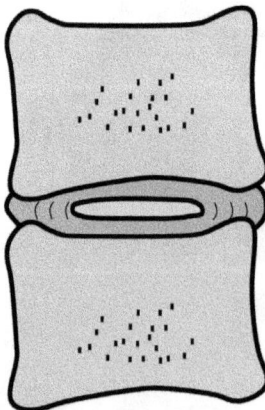

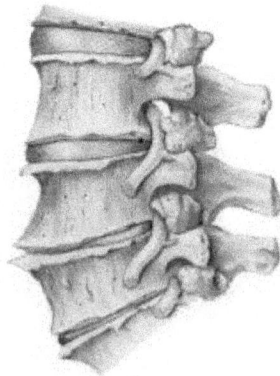

If an unusually excessive mechanical stress is applied to the back in this situation, the annulus may break and the disc under tension protrudes into the canal where the spinal cord and roots are located. Depending on the amount of disc displacement and the severity of pressure exerted on the nerves, neurological symptoms may occur. Additionally, there are times this disc dehydration occurs gradually, and the space between the vertebrae under the body's weight becomes smaller. In such cases, they are referred to as "degenerated discs.".

In the diagram above, the degenerative bulging disc is illustrated, where the nucleus becomes narrower and loses height, resulting in bulging discs. You can imagine the disc as a deflated car tyre.

In the photo next to it, there is an artistic representation of narrow intervertebral spaces with the formation of osteophytes (extra bone "spikes") at the superior and inferior parts of the vertebrae.

This latter picture indicates the degeneration of the disc and the spine in general.

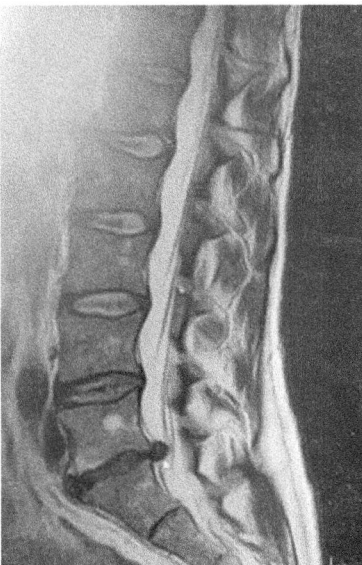

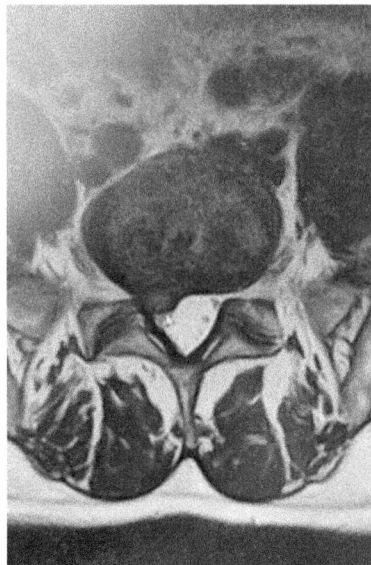

In cases where the disc is degenerative and bulging, meaning that it has lost height, there is an effect on the facet joint position, which is now "subluxed" (meaning they are not in their ideal position), resulting in "arthritic" changes, as they "grind" their surfaces in these new positions. Think of these surfaces as two millstones that are slightly displaced and need to match their surfaces again. However, this procedure creates some inflammation in the area.

On the other hand, the scan on the right shows how the nucleus of the disc is penetrating to the left after breaking the annulus and pressing on the cord and possibly one of the roots.

Despite all this, it is known that not all the loads were absorbed by the bones and discs, but the muscles play a very significant role in offloading. They are not only there to move the bones but also to support them. These muscles can be considered as additional shock absorbers on their own. Think of them as sacks of fluid that are hermetically closed and that have the ability to change the viscosity of this fluid. The higher the viscosity, the more resistance the structure has. In other words, the stronger the muscle is, the more load it can take on, something that everyone agrees with.

On top of that, the most important structure is a network of veins that exist all around the spinal cord and penetrate the bones. This network of veins is called the Plexus of Batson, as he was the one who described them. It is linked with the inferior veins that exist in the abdomen to the superior veins that exist in the thoracic cavity (chest).

These veins don't have valves as all other veins in our body.

If we increase the intra-abdominal or intra-thoracic pressure, blood is driven to these veins and the flow can be from either direction.

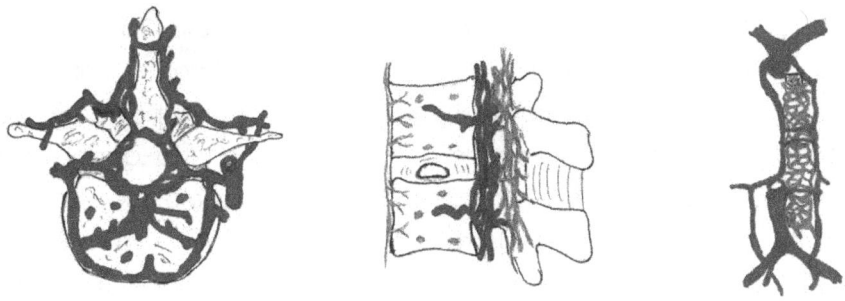

These diagrams show how the lower and higher main body veins are linked via this network of the Plexus of Batson and how this network penetrates the bones.

The mechanical properties of this network can be easily explained if the mechanism used for lifting heavy objects is explained.

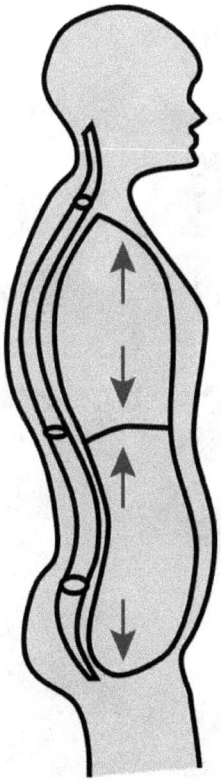

Just picture a heavy weightlifting athlete in the Olympic Games and track the movements and actions he or she does in preparation. You will observe that as soon as they are called, and after they powder their hands, they tighten their belt very tightly. This way, the intra-abdominal pressure is increased. Then, while preparing to lift, they take a deep breath and hold the air in. This way, the intra-thoracic pressure is increased. By doing this, the diaphragm, a muscle that separates the chest from the abdomen, is also immobilised under the pressure in both cavities. There is a similar action at the pelvic floor; (Incidental note: weak pelvic floor muscles can lead to bladder leakage in the case of weightlifting).

You can see in this picture how the veins around his neck are more prominent; this is due to the increased intrathoracic pressure.

It is obvious how the athlete is holding his breath in the attempt to hold the weight over his head.

At the end of the successful lifting action, and while the weights are being lowered, a cry comes out of the mouth. This cry is a violent exhale of the air held in.

You may ask, though, what is the reason I am going through this description. It is simple. With all these actions, the athlete has pushed a vast amount of blood through this venous network, the Plexus of Batson, from both directions - the abdomen and chest. The whole lifting process is done by using a hydrostatic pressure mechanism assisted by a lever mechanism. It is the same way a heavy truck is lifted at the side of the road to change a flat tyre. Usually, a hydraulic jack is used, in comparison with the means used to lift a sedan, where a jack made by arms and hinges applying mechanical lever mechanism principles is used, because the car is lighter than the truck.

The human body, as is obvious from these athletes, can lift a great deal of weight. The majority of people are not aware of the exact number of loads that can go through our body every day during our daily activities. The forces that are applied to our muscles and joints are on a scale that sometimes the mind is not able to comprehend.

There are a number of scientists who have studied and measured the loads that can go through the different parts of the body, and this part of science is called Biomechanics.

Measuring the forces that go through our spine will surprise you. An experiment was done trying to calculate the loads going through our lower back. They used an individual of average weight and height, and a weight of 20kg. This weight was positioned in different places and lifted in different ways. When the weight was placed in front of the individual's feet and they were asked to bend and lift it, they calculated that the load through the lower back was equivalent to 26kg. If the weight from the same position was lifted after the individual was asked to bend their knees and reach it with a straighter back, the load was calculated as 15kg. Then they moved the weight to an arm's length position at a lower height and lifting was ordered with an extended arm, if possible. The calculated load was equivalent to 480kg.

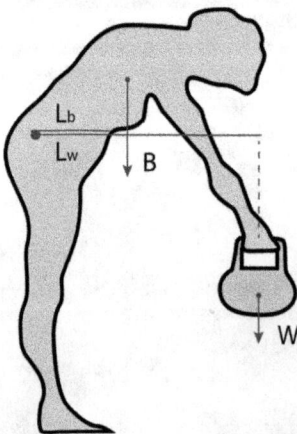

$$(L_b + B) + (L_w + W) = \text{Load (@ L5 - S1 spinal level)}$$

Thinking about the daily activities that anyone performs, this latter position is used so many times throughout the day. For example, when a mother tries to save her child by lifting them from the ground while the child is running towards the stairs, or when a cook lifts a pot full of water from the back burner of the stove. In all these actions, a very high load is placed on the spine, and then everyone wonders why they end up with back pain.

Furthermore, one should consider their own somatotype. The width of the body, when observed from the side, plays a role in the load placed on the spine. The wider the body, the longer the imaginary moment arm on which the body weight is applied while someone is in a standing position. As a result, the force applied to the muscles around the spine, especially the posterior muscles, is greater.

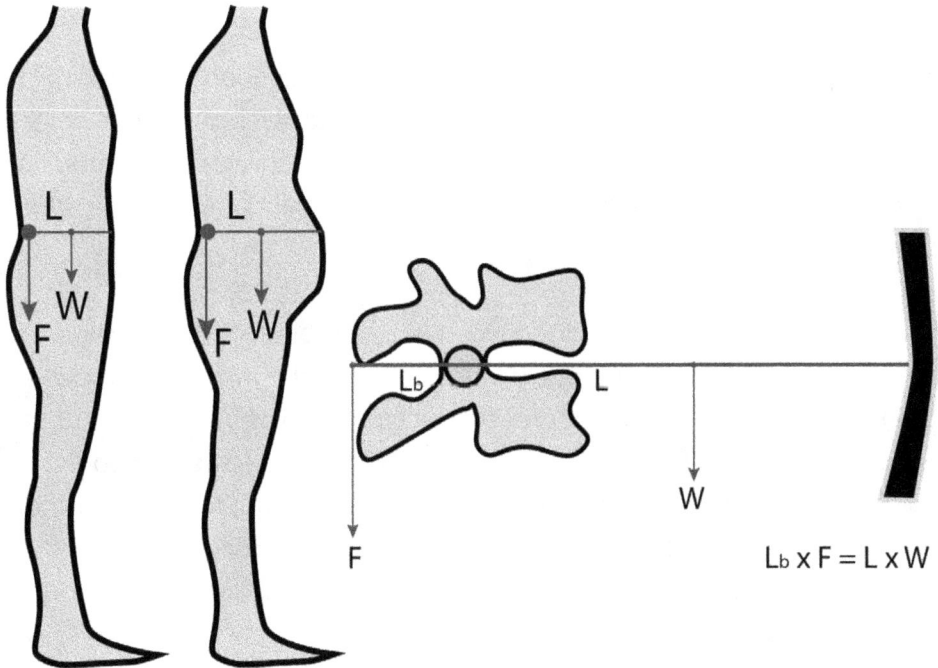

$$L_b \times F = L \times W$$

This is obvious in the diagrams seen above and how the forces can be calculated. The equation is simplified to the extreme, as other forces that can be applied to the body are not represented in the equation itself. It is clear that the wider the body, the higher the force used to keep us upright. In the case of a much wider body structure, the vector of the weight moves forward. If we take the example of a pregnant woman, the vector representing the weight can move considerably in front of the base of the body (in other words, in front of the feet), which can create a tendency for the body to topple forward. This is the reason why a pregnant woman's body changes in standing position, by hyperextending her spine (bending backwards), in order to stabilise herself while standing.

Finally, as mentioned earlier, discs are shock absorbers, but our muscles also have shock absorbing properties. Therefore, stronger muscles can offload the spine, as well as compensate for the viscosity differences mentioned above.

The shape and function of the spine can be influenced by other body pathologies. For example, hip problems such as arthritis and joint stiffness can make the symptoms of back pain more obvious, due to the effect of a muscle that links the leg directly with the pelvis and spine at the same time.

This muscle is called the Iliopsoas and is a combination of two muscles with different initial origins but a common attachment. These muscles are the Iliacus, with its belly found on the inner side of the pelvis, and the Psoas, with its belly attached to the small lateral processes and bodies of the lower vertebrae. Both bellies come together to attach with a common tendon on the inner side of the femur (thigh bone), close to the hip joint. One could simplistically say that this muscle is "linking the spine to the leg".

In the case of hip joint arthritis, the muscle can become stiffened and shortened in an attempt to protect and prevent extreme movements of the hip joint. This, in turn, pulls the spine forward and plays a crucial role in spinal loading. For an individual experiencing back pain, there is a functional change in the spine and a potential increase in symptoms.

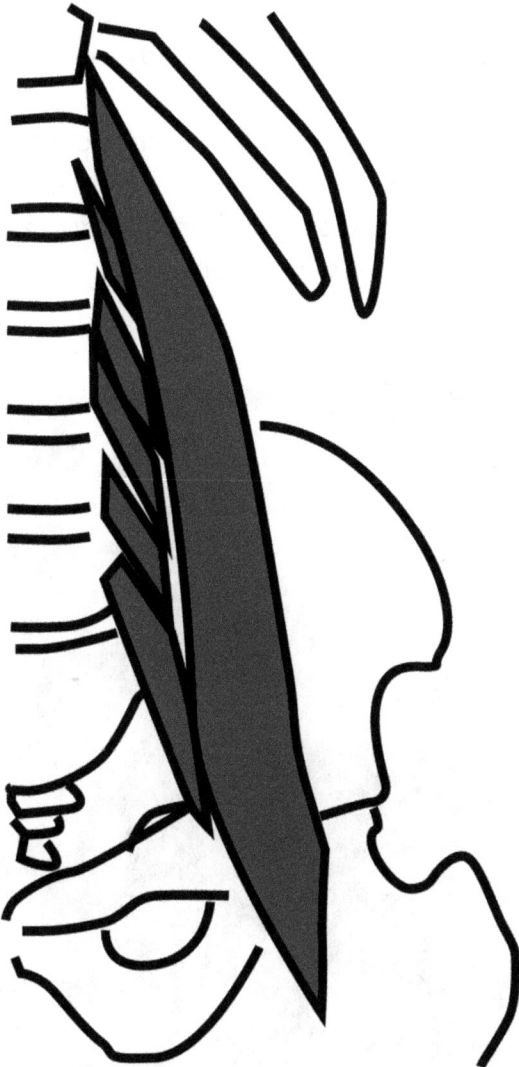

In summary, simple mechanical chronic back pain can be the result of one or many different causes that can affect a person. Understanding the mechanisms and function of our spine can help us comprehend our condition, and we could reflect by delving deep to find out what initiated our individual issue and how we can approach it in the future.

Finally, the chemistry of the body can be altered as a result of low back pain, mainly chronic pain. Here, the endocrine system will be analysed. Pain affects us physically and mentally, as already mentioned. The changes can be seen in our hormonal system. This is what I mean by endocrine. Patients' chronic pain influences their mechanical and psychological status. They fear that the pain, which is part of their life, could destroy their future. They are concentrating on their pain; they are expecting to be "hit" by it again and again, so they stay vigilant.

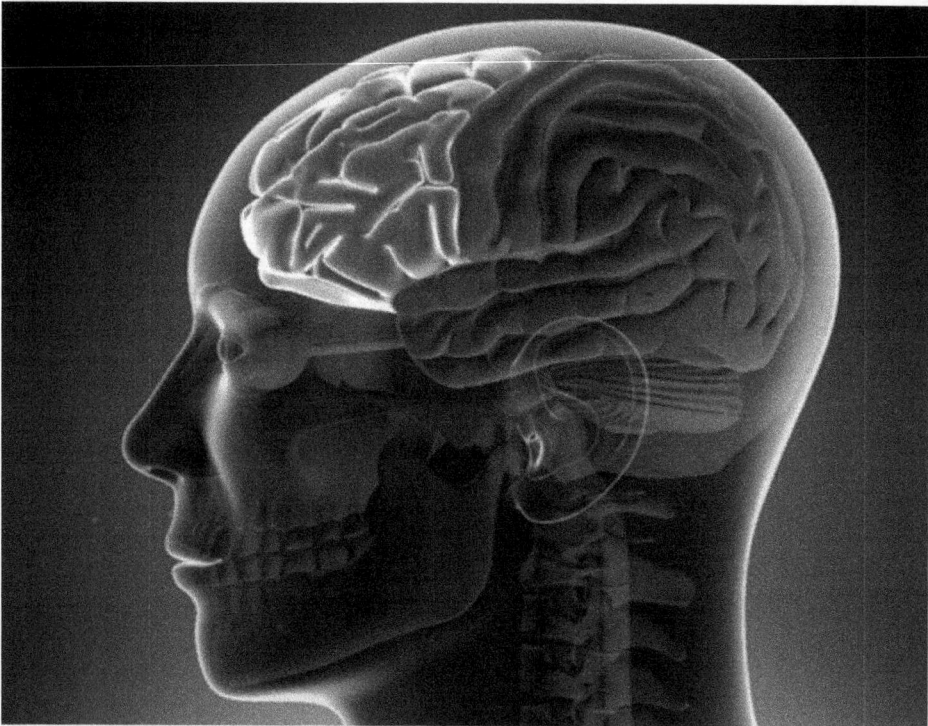

Their anxiety levels are high, and they are constantly stressed. Only negative thoughts are pouring from their mind, and they develop kinesiophobia (fear of movement). They think that if they move, the pain will come back, and the symptoms will become worse. This fear dominates their mind, and their whole being floats in a sea of uncertainty, anger, and desperation.

This situation affects their stress hormones and they, in turn, affect the primitive part of their brain initially, the pituitary gland and finally the frontal cortex of their brain where the behaviour and emotions are stored. This is the end line on the emotional stage. The emotions are imprinted on their frontal cortex and they create a new belief and habit. As soon as this is created it is moved to the cognitive part of the cortex (the brain's archive). When this information is placed in brain's archive which influences the rest of the functional brain. People are living prisoners of their own brain, which dictates all the functions and thoughts of the body.

(The diagram below shows that the initial stimulus comes to the brown area (primitive brain – Brain stem, Hypothalamus, Amygdala) and via the purple (Pituitary gland), is influencing the green (Frontal cortex), and then mapped fully in the blue area (Cortical cognitive part) of the brain).

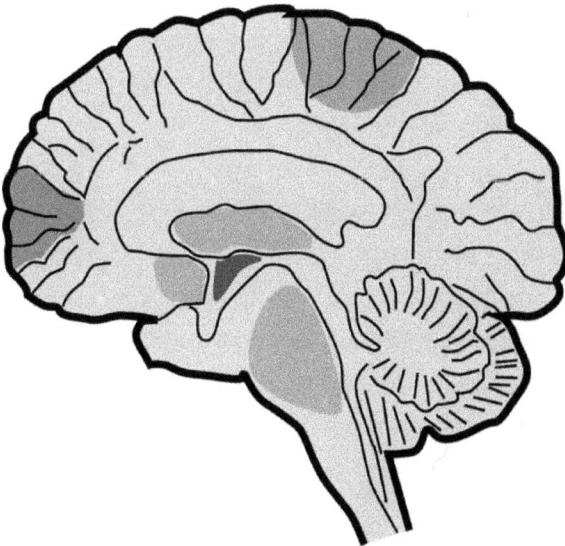

In other words, the majority of us, and I put myself in this group as a chronic low back pain sufferer, are starting to neglect ourselves. Cortisol, one of the stress hormones produced, is constantly bombarding the Hypothalamus and Pituitary Gland, the main central hormone controlling system, which are close to the primitive brain. From there, all the commands fly throughout the body, resulting in complete derangement of the rest of the hormones. This way, Thyroxin, Dopamine, and Insulin are affected. The main way of influence is Cortisol, which reduces Dopamine. Dopamine then directly influences Thyroxin by reducing it. The reduced Thyroxin makes us more "relaxed," as it tries to slow down our metabolism and fight back the effects of Cortisol. This imbalance creates Insulin resistance and, in turn, changes our dietary behaviour, producing the environment for Type 2 diabetes as it drives us to consume more food. At the same time, it affects the "inflammatory response" of the body. With the activation of this cycle, we eat more, as we are trying to affect our pleasure hormones, the endorphins. Thus, it is called comfort eating.

All this activity results in weight gain. Extra weight, as we know, is a mechanical factor that increases the load on your spine. This extra load increases your symptoms of pain and adds more tissue reaction and inflammation. Additionally, Insulin is responsible for further tissue inflammation, which can increase our symptoms. Because we are not getting better, our stress levels increase, more Cortisol is produced, and the cycle goes round and round.

As we conclude our in-depth exploration into the dynamics of flexibility, resilience, efficiency, and the endocrine system in the context of back pain, a compelling narrative emerges – one that underscores the profound influence these factors wield over the well-being of individuals within the workplace. The synthesis of flexibility, resilience, efficiency, and endocrine considerations not only serves as a strategic approach to mitigating back pain but also as a catalyst for fostering a workplace culture that prioritizes the holistic health of its workforce.

Flexibility, in both work arrangements and mindset, emerges as a cornerstone in our examination. The ability to adapt schedules, tasks, and workspaces to accommodate the needs of individuals dealing with back pain is not only a preventive measure but a fundamental aspect of creating an inclusive and supportive work environment. Flexibility allows employees to navigate their professional responsibilities while managing their back health proactively.

Resilience works as a pillar of well-being. The concept of resilience stands out as a powerful antidote to the challenges posed by back pain. Building resilience equips individuals to adapt to adversity, recover from setbacks, and maintain mental and emotional well-being. Organizations that invest in resilience training not only fortify their workforce against the psychological impacts of back pain but also foster a culture of adaptability and perseverance.

Efficiency is based on an understanding of spinal function and sustainable productivity. It has emerged as a driving force behind workplace productivity and, consequently, back health. Streamlining processes, optimising workflows, and leveraging technology contribute to a more efficient work environment. This efficiency not only enhances productivity but also allows employees the flexibility to manage their tasks in a way that aligns with their physical needs, reducing the risk of back pain associated with prolonged periods of inactivity or poor ergonomic practices.

Our exploration of the endocrine system uncovered the intricate connection between hormonal balance and back health. Stress, a common precursor to back pain, has profound effects on the endocrine system. Strategies to manage stress, such as mindfulness and wellness programs, not only benefit mental health but also contribute to hormonal equilibrium. Prioritising the endocrine well-being of employees is an investment in their overall health and resilience against the detrimental effects of chronic back pain.

The integration of flexibility, resilience, efficiency, and endocrine considerations into the workplace fabric yields a multitude of benefits. Reduced absenteeism, heightened productivity, enhanced job satisfaction, and a positive organizational culture are among the outcomes. By acknowledging the symbiotic relationship between these factors and back health, workplaces can create an environment that not only prevents and manages back pain but also nurtures the physical, mental, and emotional well-being of their employees.

In essence, our exploration advocates for a paradigm shift in how organizations approach the well-being of their workforce. By embracing flexibility, resilience, efficiency, and endocrine harmony as integral components of workplace culture, organizations can forge a path towards a future where individuals thrive both professionally and personally. The benefits extend far beyond the workplace, shaping a society where holistic health is championed, and individuals are empowered to lead fulfilling and resilient lives.

Do you remember Michael, the dynamic and driven leader? He worried about the impact on employee morale and the company's performance. His frustration grew as he struggled to find a solution that would alleviate his employees' pain.

So he decided to take a more holistic approach to address the issue of low back pain among his employees. He educated himself on the importance of flexibility, resilience, and the efficiency of muscles and the spine in managing and preventing low back pain. With this knowledge, he implemented a series of initiatives aimed at promoting flexibility and resilience in the workplace. He introduced flexible work hours and remote work options to accommodate employees' needs. In addition, he organised workshops and training sessions to educate the team on proper posture, stretching exercises, and ergonomic principles. He also invested in ergonomic equipment and furniture to support the employees' musculoskeletal health.

As a result of his efforts, he witnessed a significant improvement in employee well-being and productivity. Morale soared as employees felt more supported and empowered to take control of their health. The number of reported injuries decreased, and absenteeism due to low back pain reduced significantly. He was so proud and satisfied knowing that he had made a positive impact on his team's health and happiness.

The parts he had to attend were the importance of taking a holistic approach to address employee well-being. By considering factors such as flexibility, resilience, and the efficiency of muscles and the spine, he was able to implement effective solutions to manage and prevent low back pain.

He researched, studied, and asked experts for their help. He had to understand the different movements and how the body works. This knowledge was transmitted also to the employees and provided the tools they needed to take care of their musculoskeletal health. He empowered them to make positive changes in their daily habits and routines. The most interesting and exciting part he learned was how the own endocrine system of every single individual could help with pain management and how this system could be activated.

He understood the importance of flexibility in accommodating employees' needs and preferences. By offering flexible work hours and remote work options, he provided the team with the flexibility they needed to manage their low back pain effectively while still fulfilling their job responsibilities.

Resilience among employees was taught via workshops and training, aiming to help them cope with the challenges of low back pain. This way, they were equipped with the skills they needed to bounce back from setbacks and stay motivated and engaged in their work.

The creation of a supportive and healthy work environment was an ongoing process. Because of this, there was a commitment to regularly evaluate and adjust these programs to make sure they remained up to date, effective, and relevant as the company grew and evolved.

Finally, by implementing all the above, meaning flexibility, resilience, and understanding the efficiency of muscles and spine, it was possible to significantly improve employee well-being, productivity, and morale, leading to positive outcomes for both the employees and the company as a whole.

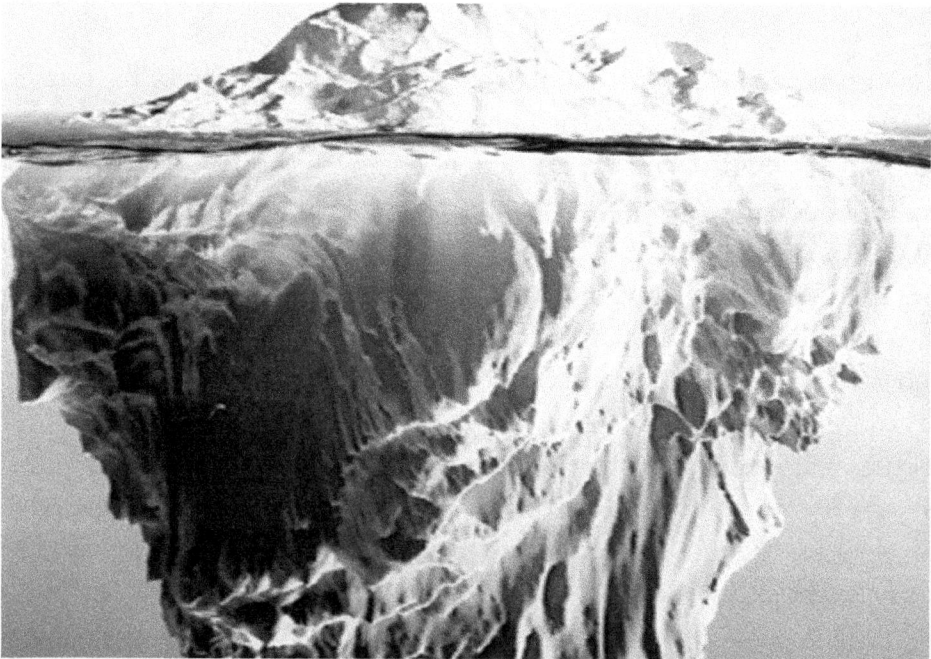

# 3

## CHAPTER

## ASSISTANCE

But what is ASSISTANCE and how is it linked to low back pain and work? What is its meaning?

Assistance refers to the act of providing help, support, or aid to someone in need. It involves offering assistance to individuals or groups to facilitate a task, address a challenge, or meet a specific need. It can take various forms, including physical help, guidance, advice, resources, or any other form of support that contributes to the well-being or success of the recipient. Assistance involves taking action to assist others in achieving a goal, overcoming an obstacle, or addressing a problem. It may include both tangible actions and emotional support. It can be voluntary, where individuals offer help without being asked, or it can be solicited, where someone explicitly seeks aid or support. The nature of assistance can vary based on the context. It may involve physical help, financial support, guidance, mentorship, counselling, or any other form of aid relevant to the specific situation.

When people provide assistance, it often requires having empathy and understanding of the needs and challenges faced by the person seeking help. They need to be attentive to the other person's situation, and this helps tailor the assistance appropriately.

In many cases, assistance involves collaboration between individuals or entities working together to achieve a common goal or address a shared concern. Assistance has a lot to do with communication within a business environment, and it is clear that we can see some examples of everyday activities in different industries, such as helping someone carry heavy objects, offering guidance on a complex task, providing emotional support during difficult times, contributing resources to a charitable cause, or extending a helping hand to someone in distress. Assistance plays a vital role in fostering a sense of community, building relationships, and promoting collective well-being. Whether in personal relationships, professional settings, or broader societal contexts, the act of assisting others contributes to a supportive and interconnected community. But quite commonly, this necessary communication, camaraderie, and looking after one another is missing, and such issues can lead to injuries within the company's premises. This is something that can lead to the loss of people, loss of productivity, and increased costs, and within these costs could be compensations. It is reported that the average compensation for low back pain injury is about £40,000.00, although there are reports of a figure of £600,000.00.

And I will ask all the business leaders: do they have this kind of money ready to be burned instead of investing them within their business?

Business leaders who underwent the S.A.F.E. Working Ways programme learned how to arrange the different projects, energise the employees, help the smooth flow running the tasks, and create a safe working environment.

This system incorporates the steps of S.A.F.E'? creating a safe environment, Arrangement, meaning the way of organising the different tasks, Flow

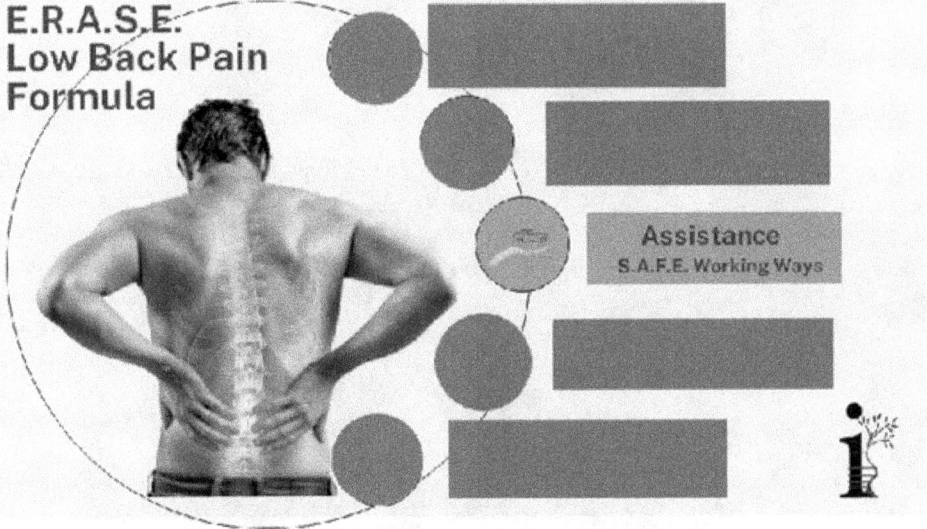

E.R.A.S.E.
Low Back Pain
Formula

Assistance
S.A.F.E. Working Ways

as the way of calm and unobstructed development of all activities, and Energy, which analyses the ways the workforce is pumped and performs better, resulting in greater productivity.

Let's start with Safety.

But what does Safety means?

I believe that everyone knows what safety is. Safety refers to the state of being free from harm, danger, or the risk of injury. It encompasses the measures, practices, and conditions that are implemented or present to prevent accidents, injuries, or any form of harm to individuals, property, or the environment. Safety is a fundamental consideration in various contexts, including workplaces, homes, public spaces, transportation, and recreational activities.

Safety involves taking proactive measures to prevent accidents, incidents, or injuries from occurring. This can include the implementation of safety

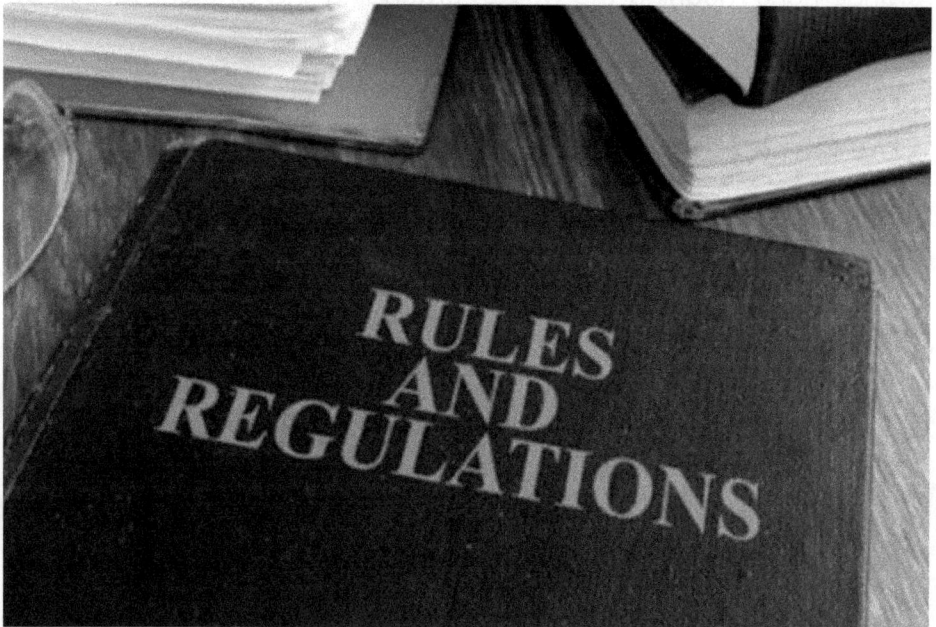

protocols, guidelines, and the use of protective equipment. To be safe, someone has to identify and mitigate potential risks. This is a crucial aspect. It involves assessing potential hazards, implementing controls, and creating environments that minimise the likelihood of accidents.

To ensure that everybody is safe within the company, people have to comply with and adhere to safety regulations, standards, and best practices.

This is essential to maintain a safe environment. It can involve following industry-specific guidelines, legal requirements, and established safety protocols.

To create a safe work environment, everyone needs to be prepared to respond to emergencies or unexpected events. This involves having plans, procedures, and resources in place to address crises and minimise harm in the event of an incident.

Promoting safety often includes educating individuals on potential hazards, safe practices, and emergency procedures. Training programs help individuals understand and implement safety measures effectively.

All these regulations, guidelines, and training have to incorporate an ongoing process that requires regular evaluation and improvement. This may involve reviewing incidents, analysing near-misses, and updating safety protocols to enhance overall safety performance.

To maintain a safe workplace, individuals play a role in their own safety by exercising personal responsibility. This includes following safety guidelines, using protective equipment, and being aware of potential risks in their environment. In the workplace, safety focuses on creating conditions that protect employees from workplace hazards and ensure their well-being. Occupational safety measures include proper training, the use of safety equipment, and adherence to regulations. On top of that, safety considerations extend to the protection of the environment. This involves practices that prevent pollution, minimise environmental impact, and promote sustainability. This extends to public safety. Public safety involves measures taken by governments and communities to protect the well-being of the public. This can include law enforcement, emergency services, and infrastructure planning to ensure the safety of citizens.

So, safety is a multi-faceted concept that requires a combination of planning, awareness, and adherence to established guidelines to create secure environments for individuals, communities, and organisations.

Very frequently, people do not follow any of these aspects and do not even create safety regulations within the workplace. This may result in injuries, and a common issue is low back pain.

On these grounds, what do you think is the connection between safety and back pain?

Safety and back pain are two distinct but interconnected topics, especially when it comes to physical well-being. But what does anybody have to consider regarding safety and back pain?

It is analysed and the initial topic is the understanding of body mechanics and assistance that is necessary. That includes training for people to learn the correct lifting techniques and the correct posture the body has to have. When lifting objects, it is necessary to use proper body mechanics. Bend at the knees, not at the waist, and lift using the legs, keeping the object close to the body. Also, it is necessary to maintain good posture, whether sitting or standing, to reduce stress on the spine. Sit up straight and avoid slouching.

Ergonomics have already been analysed, and the company must ensure that the workspace is ergonomically designed. The chair, desk, and computer should be at the correct height to prevent strain on the back. If feasible, consider using an adjustable desk or workstation that allows for switching between sitting and standing positions throughout the day.

If business leaders are caring, they may extend the training and information given to their employees by educating them on how to apply correct ergonomics even at home. For example, they can teach employees how to choose the correct mattress and pillow that provide adequate support for the spine. A mattress that is too soft or too firm can contribute to back pain.

The use of assistive devices or tools, such as dollies or carts, can reduce the need for heavy lifting.

If possible, alternate between tasks that involve different body movements to avoid prolonged stress on the lower back.

In addition to the above, employees should be educated about the importance of regular exercise. Help them engage in regular exercise, including activities that strengthen the core muscles that support the spine. Incorporate stretching and flexibility exercises into the exercise routine to improve the range of motion and reduce the risk of muscle strains. This can help prevent back pain and improve overall safety by maintaining a healthy, strong body. Diet and control of the Body Mass Index (BMI) by maintaining a healthy weight to reduce the load on the spine are paramount. Excess weight can contribute to back pain and increase the risk of injuries.

Something that very few people stress is the importance of correct footwear. Why do you think this is important? Let's go back and remember what a disc is. Do we agree that it is a shock absorber? People with low back pain have limitations in this shock absorption, and comfortable, supportive shoes with shock-absorbing insoles or soles can help and also promote proper alignment and reduction of stress on your back.

On top of everything, people have to take care of their body care, and this is very important. It begins with a great night of relaxation. People must ensure that they get enough sleep and allow their body adequate time to rest and recover. Lack of sleep and overexertion can contribute to back pain. Hydration is another important part of our existence. If a person is well hydrated, it is believed that they keep the intervertebral discs properly hydrated. Dehydration can affect the fluid-filled discs in the spine, leading to discomfort.

It is known that most of the time during our lives, we are sitting. If the job involves prolonged periods of sitting, someone needs to take regular breaks to stand, stretch, and move around. Sitting for extended periods can contribute to back pain.

Remember, everyone's body is unique, and what works for one person may not work for another. It's essential to pay attention to your body, make adjustments as needed, and seek professional advice if you have concerns about back pain or safety issues.

The next step to be discussed is Arrangement.

What do you think is the meaning of Arrangement?

Arrangement refers to the organisation, placement, or configuration of elements or objects in a particular order or pattern. It involves intentionally positioning or grouping things to achieve a specific purpose, enhance functionality, or create a desired aesthetic. Arrangements can be found in various contexts, including physical spaces, events, compositions, or plans. The term is versatile and can apply to diverse situations, encompassing both tangible and abstract aspects.

Arrangement implies a deliberate order or organisation of elements. It involves structuring components in a systematic way to achieve a particular result or effect, or creating optimal functionality or harmony around the working person. Arrangement can be a means of communication or expression. For instance, the arrangement of words in a sentence, the arrangement of musical notes in a composition, or the arrangement of elements in a visual display all convey messages or emotions. Arrangements can be flexible or rigid, depending on the context. Some arrangements may allow for adjustments, while others may follow strict guidelines or rules. Low back pain sufferers may evidently benefit from a flexible arrangement.

It is frequently obvious that such an arrangement is not happening, resulting in a lack of balance and communication. This may create confusion, and confusion is the root of injuries.

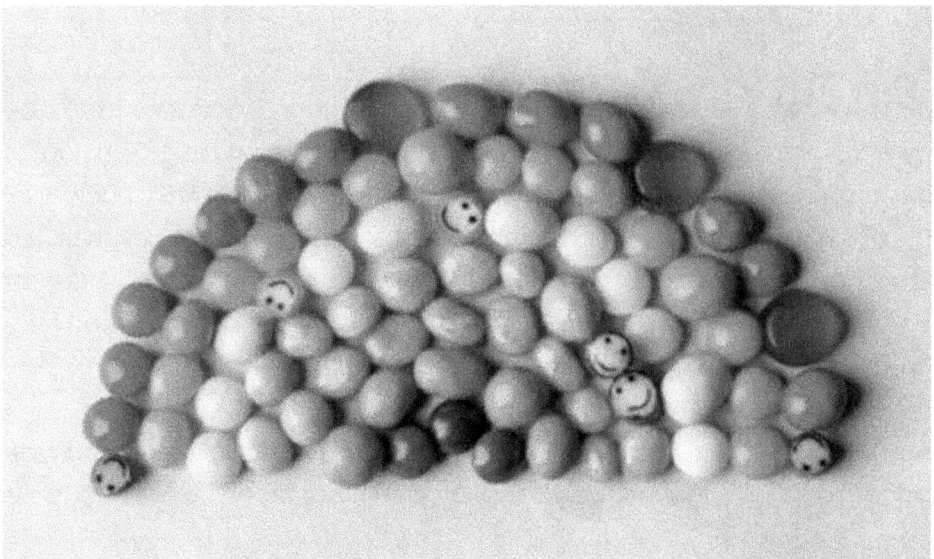

This constant link of communication and organisation in a flexible environment will need to be centred on the employee. To create a successful working place for everyone, but mainly for the low back pain sufferer, with this person at the centre, the activities need to be prioritised.

Managing low back pain in a working environment requires a thoughtful approach to prioritise activities that support healing, reduce strain, and maintain productivity. A low back pain sufferer needs to inform the employer about the symptoms and discuss potential accommodations or adjustments to the work environment. Open communication is the key to receiving the necessary support. Additionally, open communication with colleagues about their condition and limitations can be beneficial. Seeking support from the immediate team of working colleagues can ensure a collaborative and understanding work environment.

It is important to prioritise activities that reduce strain on the lower back, improve overall well-being, and promote healing. Some of the suggested activities for someone experiencing low back pain are pain management using medications given by a healthcare professional, such as a primary care physician or orthopaedic specialist. Other people who may help are physical therapists, chiropractors, or osteopaths.

As a first step, rest and avoidance of aggravating activities could be helpful. That means prioritizing activities and organizing tasks. The goal of this arranged prioritisation is controlled healing of the back. It's necessary to avoid activities that may worsen pain or strain the lower back muscles. This may involve modifying daily routines and avoiding heavy lifting or prolonged sitting. Mind-Body Practices, such as yoga or tai chi, can help improve flexibility, reduce stress, and promote overall well-being.

However, an ergonomic evaluation and equipment assessment must be performed. If the job involves lifting, proper lifting techniques need to be followed. Techniques such as bending at the knees, keeping the object close to the body, and avoiding twisting while lifting are necessary. If the job involves a mix of activities, alternating between tasks that require different body movements may be considered. This can prevent overuse of specific muscles and reduce the risk of exacerbating low back pain.

A management leader can delegate tasks that involve heavy lifting or extensive physical strain to multiple members of the team. Additionally, they should ensure that responsibilities are distributed among team members to minimise the risk of exacerbating back pain.

Regular breaks need to be taken to allow for standing, stretching, and moving around. Prolonged sitting can exacerbate low back pain, so incorporating movement breaks is crucial.

A low back pain sufferer, during the acute phase of symptoms, needs to be gradually reintroduced to normal activities, such as work responsibilities and daily chores, as their back pain improves. It's important to listen to the body and avoid pushing oneself too hard too soon.

Once the back pain has improved, it is necessary for the person to continue with a maintenance plan that includes regular exercise, proper posture, and other lifestyle adjustments to prevent future episodes of low

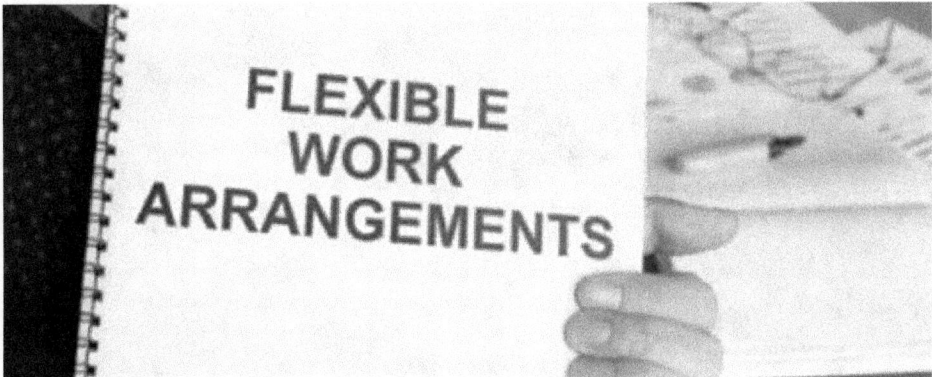

FLEXIBLE WORK ARRANGEMENTS

back pain. If necessary, exploration of flexible work arrangements, such as telecommuting or adjusting work hours, if feasible has to be explored. This can provide the employee with more control over the work environment and schedule.

It's important to customise these recommendations based on the specific job responsibilities and medical condition. Additionally, ongoing communication with the healthcare provider and employer is crucial to ensure a supportive and accommodating work environment.

The next element to go under the microscope is flow.

In a general sense, flow refers to the state of optimal experience where individuals are fully absorbed and immersed in an activity, experiencing intense focus, enjoyment, and a sense of being in the zone. This concept was introduced by psychologist Mihaly Csikszentmihalyi and is often associated with a state of heightened concentration and intrinsic motivation. He describes flow as the ecstasy that pushes your life towards a more meaningful way. According to his teachings, an ethical business owner / CEO describes success as something that promotes care and assistance to others and at the same time makes them feel happy while working on it. This is what they project to their employees. But just these are not enough to make them successful.

Anita Roddick, founder of the cosmetic firm Body Shop, says that to be a successful worker, one has to be filled with passion that comes out from this person doing their best and having flow while they are working.

Sony's founder Masaru Ibuka says that he wanted to create a company "where engineers can feel the joy of technological innovation, be aware of their mission to society, and work to their heart's content".

To achieve flow, an employee has to be focused, concentrated, and completely involved in what they are doing. They need to have complete inner clarity by knowing what needs to be done and how well it has to be performed. They should be clear about what is possible and if their skills are adequate for the task they were placed to perform. Additionally, they should have a sense of serenity by feeling safe and secure, without any worries. On top of that, they need to be thoroughly focused on the present moment in such a way that the hours pass by, feeling like mere seconds as time is forgotten and distractions fade into the background. Focus has to be effortless, meaning that despite the intensity of focus, individuals in a flow state often describe the experience as one of effortless action. People in a flow state often report a diminished awareness of their surroundings and a temporary loss of self-consciousness. The sense of time may also be altered, with individuals perceiving time as passing quickly. They feel a sense of mastery over the activity, and the skills required for the task are deployed effortlessly. On top of that, they have to have internal motivation to such a degree that the result of their task is their own reward. Flow experiences are intrinsically rewarding, providing a sense of satisfaction and fulfilment. The enjoyment comes from the process of the activity itself, rather than external rewards or recognition.

As it is evident, flow and efficiency at work are interlinked and crucial for productivity, job satisfaction, and overall success. However, to achieve a constant flow, the fulfilment of some parameters would be necessary. Firstly, clear and achievable goals and priorities must be set. These objectives need to be communicated to the team clearly, as it will be necessary to ensure that everyone is aligned and working towards common outcomes.

Effective communication with open dialogue, active listening, reflection, and constructive feedback needs to exist to minimise misunderstandings and promote a collaborative environment. Unnecessary steps or bottlenecks in workflows need to be identified and eliminated. Streamlined processes reduce redundancy and save time, enabling a smoother workflow. The tasks have to be delegated according to team members' strengths and expertise. This ensures that each person is working on tasks they are well-suited for, maximizing efficiency. Teaching and encouragement to achieve effective prioritisation and time management skills have to be paramount. This includes setting deadlines, breaking down tasks, and focusing on high-priority items first. Despite this, it will be necessary to offer and promote flexible work arrangements, such as remote work or flexible hours, to accommodate different working styles and individual preferences, ultimately boosting productivity.

This will be easily performed if tools and technologies that enhance efficiency are implemented. Project management software, communication tools, and automation can significantly improve workflow and collaboration. Employees have to be encouraged to continuously follow ongoing Training and Development programmes in order to enhance their skills and knowledge. A well-trained workforce is likely to be more efficient in handling their tasks. Employees must not work constantly without any breaks. Research suggests that brief breaks can help maintain focus and prevent burnout, ultimately improving overall efficiency. Designate areas where team members can easily come together to brainstorm, discuss ideas, and solve problems collaboratively have to be created.

To facilitate the flow of the workforce, a system to recognise and reward their contributions needs to become the norm. This will reinforce them in a positive way and boost their morale and motivation, ultimately leading to increased productivity.

Prioritise employee well-being by promoting a healthy work-life balance. A well-rested and physically and mentally healthy workforce is more likely to be productive and efficient.

A caring business owner is necessary to conduct regular performance reviews, providing feedback, setting goals, and addressing any challenges. This helps employees understand expectations and areas for improvement, fostering a culture of continuous improvement. Flow is more likely to occur when individuals have clear goals and receive immediate feedback on their performance. The task should provide a balance between challenge and skill, with the challenge level matching or slightly exceeding the individual's skill level. This delicate balance contributes to a sense of engagement and enjoyment.

Encourage employees to share ideas for enhancing processes and be open to making adjustments based on feedback. This has been proven to be a successful tool in the hands of CEOs who want their company to be successful and thriving. This technique promotes a flexible and adaptable

approach and fosters necessary change that allows the team to quickly adjust to new challenges and capitalize on opportunities, maintaining a steady flow of work. Additionally, if unnecessary interruptions are minimised and "quiet hours" or specific times for focused work are established, employees can concentrate without constant disruptions, ultimately expanding the company's productivity.

It is evident that by caring for all people in your company, without dividing or excluding anyone despite their health issues, such as those suffering from low back pain, and incorporating their individual abilities in a constructive and positive way, the future of any company can reach higher levels.

To further clarify how back pain sufferers can manage their pain using flow, studies have shown that flow experiences involve deep concentration and immersion in an activity. This intense focus can act as a distraction, reducing the individual's awareness of pain. When fully engaged in a flow state, the brain may allocate fewer resources to processing pain signals, resulting in a perceived reduction in pain intensity. Individuals in flow are fully engaged in the present moment, with distractions fading into the background. Flow entails a seamless merging of action and awareness, where individuals are fully involved in what they are doing and actions unfold spontaneously.

It has been found that senses such as Control and Arousal, and to a lesser degree Relaxation, can help people reach the state of Flow, unlike the senses of Anxiety, Worry, Apathy, and Boredom. Individuals in flow often lose track of time, experiencing a distortion in their perception of the passing time. This can result in extended periods of engagement without a sense of fatigue.

But how can Flow help employees with back pain?

Engaging in activities that induce a state of flow can have potential benefits for individuals experiencing low back pain. Flow experiences promote mental and emotional well-being, and the positive effects on mood, focus, and relaxation can contribute to pain management.

Flow activities often involve a sense of challenge and accomplishment. Engaging in challenging yet achievable tasks can trigger the release of endorphins, which are natural pain-relieving chemicals produced by the body. Endorphins act as neurotransmitters that interact with receptors in the brain, reducing pain perception and promoting a positive mood.

These flow experiences are associated with positive emotions and a sense of well-being. Activities that induce flow can help improve mood and reduce stress, which are factors known to influence the perception of pain. Lower stress levels may contribute to overall relaxation and a more positive mental state, potentially easing low back pain.

They often lead to a state of relaxation, and this relaxation can extend to the muscles. Reduced muscle tension can be particularly beneficial for individuals with low back pain, as muscle tightness and spasms are common contributors to discomfort. Engaging in flow-inducing activities may help relax the muscles and alleviate tension.

They often involve a strong connection between mental focus and physical actions. This mind-body connection can enhance overall awareness and mindfulness. By being attuned to body movements and sensations during flow activities, individuals may develop a greater sense of control over their body, potentially influencing pain perception.

Many activities that induce flow involve physical movement. Regular physical activity is associated with numerous health benefits, including improved musculoskeletal health. When an individual is engaging in flow-inducing activities that incorporate movement, it can contribute to overall physical well-being and may have positive effects on the lower back.

It's important to note that while flow experiences can provide relief and distraction from low back pain, they may not be a substitute for addressing the underlying causes of the pain. Individuals experiencing chronic or severe low back pain should seek medical advice for a comprehensive assessment and appropriate management strategies, which may include a combination of medical interventions, physical therapy, and ergonomic adjustments.

Some general activities that promote flow include sports, playing musical instruments, writing, painting, coding, or any task that requires skill and concentration. The concept of flow has been applied in various fields, including education, work, and leisure, to enhance performance, creativity, and overall well-being.

As mentioned above, the need for inclusiveness and focus is necessary to keep everyone happy, but on top of that, employees need to be motivated. This motivation, this energy, is something everyone needs to carry out their tasks.

But how can you energise low back pain sufferers? How do they need to leap over all their physical and mental obstacles?

But what do I mean by "energise"?

To energise, means to give someone or something energy, vitality, or enthusiasm. It can also refer to the process of providing power or activating something to make it operate. Energising can involve reviving or invigorating someone's spirit or revitalising a system or process. It's all about infusing vigour, excitement, or power into a person.

To energise a low back pain sufferer at work involves creating a supportive environment that encourages physical well-being, reduces discomfort, and enhances overall energy levels. To achieve this, someone needs to ensure that the individual's workspace is ergonomically designed. A comfortable chair with lumbar support, an adjustable desk, and proper monitor placement can contribute to reduced back strain and increased comfort. It is necessary to encourage them to move regularly by promoting regular breaks for stretching and movement. Gentle exercises or stretches specifically designed to alleviate low back pain can be suggested and introduced. Ask them to set reminders for short breaks to encourage regular movement throughout the day. The ergonomic chairs mentioned above need to be adjustable with multiple seating options, such as a stability ball or a chair with dynamic features. This allows the individual to change positions and engage their core muscles, promoting better posture and reducing strain on the lower back. Supply lumbar support cushions for chairs. These cushions can help maintain the natural curve of the spine and alleviate discomfort in the lower back.

A designated comfortable break area where employees can relax can be introduced. This area needs to have ergonomic chairs, cushions, or even a designated space for brief rest periods. The pains can create stress and fatigue. Allow flexibility in seating arrangements. If possible, permit the individual to choose a chair or alternative seating option that provides the most comfort and support for their back.

Promote mindfulness during these breaks. It is found that deep breathing exercises, meditation, or short walks help reduce stress and increase energy levels. Employee wellness programs that focus on physical well-being are also beneficial. This may include on-site fitness classes, workshops on back health, or access to wellness resources.

Some scholars indicated that dehydration can contribute to feelings of fatigue, so encourage all employees, and in particular low back pain sufferers, to stay hydrated as this is essential for their overall well-being. The minimum volume is two litres of water per day, although up to four litres can improve their condition as it is healthier.

Natural light has also been shown to positively impact mood and energy levels. If possible, the workstation/desk should be positioned near a window. It is found that for right-handed people, the light should come from their right, and for left-handed people, it should come from their left. This way, the body does not cast a shadow over the desk, as there is a tendency for the body to lean over the desk.

The benefits of flexible work arrangements have already been discussed. Working from home or adjusting work hours can allow individuals to manage their energy levels and work in a way that accommodates their needs.

Education can raise awareness among colleagues about the challenges faced by someone with low back pain. This will encourage empathy and understanding, fostering a supportive workplace culture. Health professionals and physiotherapists can provide this information and examples of resources related to managing and preventing back pain. Physiotherapists are known to provide physical support and promote

fitness. Regular exercise, tailored to the individual's capabilities, can contribute to improved energy levels and overall well-being. Health providers can also support chronic back pain sufferers not only physically but also mentally. Employees who are suffering from back pain should be acknowledged for their commitment to work despite dealing with back pain. This can boost morale and motivation.

By implementing all of this, employers, business owners, and CEOs can create a workplace that energises and supports individuals dealing with low back pain. It is essential to tailor these approaches to the specific needs and preferences of the individual, considering their unique circumstances and the nature of their work.

In our extensive analysis of the factors of safety, arrangement, flow, and energy and their impact on back pain within the workplace, a compelling narrative emerges—one that emphasises not only the importance of physical considerations but also the holistic integration of workplace design and energy dynamics. As we conclude our exploration, it is clear that creating a workplace that prioritises safety, thoughtful arrangement, efficient flow, and positive energy not only serves as a preventive measure against back pain but also as a catalyst for fostering a thriving and productive professional environment.

Safety emerges as the bedrock upon which a healthy workplace is built. From ergonomic considerations to creating a hazard-free environment, prioritising safety is not just a regulatory requirement but a fundamental commitment to the well-being of employees. A safe workplace not only minimises the risk of back injuries but also fosters a culture of trust, reliability, and overall job satisfaction.

The arrangement of workspaces and the design of ergonomic solutions play a pivotal role in preventing back pain. Thoughtful arrangement, including adjustable desks, supportive chairs, and proper workstation layouts, contribute to an ergonomic harmony that supports good posture and reduces strain on the back. Such arrangements not only mitigate the risk of back pain but also enhance overall comfort and productivity.

In conclusion, our exploration advocates for a comprehensive and integrated approach to workplace design—one that goes beyond the physical aspects and considers the holistic well-being of individuals. By prioritising safety, arranging workspaces thoughtfully, optimising workflow, and fostering positive energy dynamics, workplaces can lay the foundation for a future where individuals not only thrive professionally but also experience a profound sense of physical and emotional well-being. The benefits extend far beyond the workplace, shaping a society where holistic health is championed, and individuals are empowered to lead fulfilling and resilient lives.

# 4

## CHAPTER

## SERENITY

What SERENITY is and how is serenity and how does it affect those who suffer from low back pain?

Serenity refers to a state of tranquillity, calmness, and peacefulness. It is the harmony between different physical or mental conditions. It is the quality or condition of being free from disturbance, agitation, or turmoil. When someone experiences serenity, they typically feel a sense of inner peace and harmony, often accompanied by a quiet and undisturbed state of mind. Serenity is associated with a calm and harmonious environment, both externally and internally, fostering a sense of balance and contentment. It is a state often sought after for relaxation, meditation, and a general sense of well-being.

The relationship between back pain and serenity involves understanding how physical well-being and emotional calmness can influence each other. While back pain is often a physical issue, managing stress and promoting serenity can positively impact one's experience of pain.
High stress levels can contribute to muscle tension, which may exacerbate back pain. Finding serenity through relaxation techniques, meditation, or mindfulness can help reduce stress and alleviate muscle tension in the back.

The mind and body are interconnected, and emotional well-being can influence physical health. Practices that promote serenity, such as yoga or

tai chi, often emphasize the mind-body connection, leading to improved overall health, including back health.

Stress and anxiety can heighten the perception of pain. By cultivating serenity and reducing stress, individuals may experience a lower sensitivity to pain, making back discomfort more manageable.

Serenity and relaxation practices contribute to better sleep quality. Adequate and restful sleep is essential for the body's healing processes, potentially alleviating back pain or preventing its exacerbation. Serenity is harmony.

Harmony and effective communication can play a positive role in managing and alleviating low back pain. The relationship between these elements and back pain involves several interconnected factors. Stress reduction is the first one as harmony in personal and professional relationships can contribute to stress reduction. Chronic stress is known to exacerbate back pain, so fostering a harmonious environment can help minimise stress levels and alleviate its impact on physical well-being. Positive and harmonious relationships often contribute to emotional well-being. Emotional health is closely linked to how individuals perceive and manage pain. Feeling supported and emotionally secure can positively influence the experience of low back pain. Healthy communication fosters a supportive environment.

Having a strong support system, where individuals can openly discuss their challenges and receive understanding and encouragement, can positively impact the coping mechanisms associated with low back pain. Effective communication and harmony in relationships can contribute to reduced tension and anxiety. Muscle tension and anxiety can exacerbate back pain, so creating an atmosphere of understanding and cooperation may help alleviate these factors. In a harmonious and communicative environment, individuals may be more likely to approach health issues, including back pain, as a team. Collaborative efforts in adopting healthy lifestyle habits, such as regular exercise and stress reduction techniques, can contribute to overall well-being. A harmonious workplace environment, characterised by positive communication and mutual respect, can reduce job-related stress and contribute to overall job satisfaction. This, in turn, may positively influence the management of back pain for employees. The mind-body connection is crucial in managing pain. Harmony and positive communication contribute to a more balanced mental state, potentially reducing the perception of pain and improving overall well-being. Open communication within a harmonious environment can encourage the adoption of healthy habits. This may include promoting regular physical activity, proper ergonomic practices, and stress-reducing activities that collectively contribute to managing and preventing low back pain. Addressing conflicts through effective communication strategies can prevent the build-up of tension and stress, which can be detrimental to back health. Resolving conflicts in a positive and constructive manner contributes to a harmonious atmosphere. Healthy relationships and effective communication provide a platform for discussing and implementing coping strategies. Sharing effective coping mechanisms for managing stress and pain can contribute to a more harmonious and supportive environment.

While harmony and communication can contribute positively to managing low back pain, it's important to note that individual experiences and pain management strategies vary. Seeking professional advice from healthcare providers, including physical therapists and pain specialists, can provide personalized guidance tailored to individual needs and conditions. Additionally, open communication with family members, colleagues, and healthcare professionals is crucial in creating a supportive network for individuals dealing with low back pain.

Serenity can serve as a positive coping mechanism for dealing with chronic conditions like back pain. Developing healthy coping strategies, such as mindfulness or guided imagery, can contribute to a more serene mindset in the face of physical challenges.

Approaches that address both physical and emotional aspects can be effective in managing back pain. Techniques such as biofeedback or progressive muscle relaxation may promote serenity while helping individuals gain better control over their pain.

Practices like deep breathing, progressive muscle relaxation, or guided imagery are relaxation techniques that can promote serenity and alleviate both physical and emotional tension, potentially improving the experience of back pain.

Adopting a serene and positive outlook on life can lead to healthier lifestyle choices. This may include maintaining a balanced diet, engaging in regular exercise, and avoiding behaviours that could exacerbate back pain.

Serenity can be fostered through therapeutic interventions such as massage, acupuncture, or spa treatments. These practices not only provide physical relief but also contribute to a sense of calm and well-being.

Cognitive-behavioural therapy techniques can help individuals develop a more serene mindset by addressing negative thought patterns and promoting healthier perspectives, potentially reducing the impact of chronic pain.

Cognitive-behavioural approaches to controlling back pain involve strategies that address both the cognitive (thoughts, beliefs, attitudes) and behavioural (actions, habits) aspects of an individual's experience with pain. These approaches aim to empower individuals to better manage and cope with back pain by changing negative thought patterns, promoting healthier behaviours, and enhancing overall well-being. Cognitive restructuring, which is based on the identification and challenge of negative thought patterns related to back pain, helps individuals develop a more balanced and constructive mindset.

Keeping a journal allows someone to track pain experiences, identifying patterns, triggers, and the impact of thoughts and emotions on pain perception. This process helps individuals gain insights into the factors influencing their pain experience.

Relaxation methods such as deep breathing, progressive muscle relaxation, or guided imagery can help reduce muscle tension, alleviate stress, and promote overall relaxation, which can contribute to pain relief.

The introduction of mindfulness practices cultivates present-moment awareness. Mindfulness meditation and related techniques can enhance pain acceptance, reduce anxiety, and improve overall well-being. When individuals are gradually exposed to activities or movements, they may be avoiding due to fear of pain.

A person has to set realistic and achievable goals related to physical activity, function, and overall well-being. Breaking down larger goals into smaller, manageable steps can provide a sense of accomplishment and motivation.

When individuals build a supportive network of friends, family, or support groups, they achieve a way through which social support can play a crucial role in coping with chronic pain and maintaining a positive outlook.

It's important to note that these approaches are often most effective when implemented as part of a comprehensive pain management plan, which may also include medical interventions, physical therapy, and lifestyle modifications. Individuals experiencing chronic back pain should consult with healthcare professionals for personalized guidance and treatment options.

On top of that, while cultivating serenity can complement the management of back pain, individual responses to pain and stress vary. Consultation with healthcare professionals, including physical therapists, pain specialists, and mental health professionals, can help develop a comprehensive approach to managing both physical discomfort and emotional well-being.

But what is the relationship between serenity, time, and low back pain?

The connection lies in the potential impact of stress, lifestyle, and time on one's well-being, particularly in the context of back pain.

Serenity, or a state of calm and peace, is associated with stress reduction. Chronic stress can contribute to muscle tension, inflammation, and exacerbate conditions like low back pain. Achieving serenity through relaxation techniques, mindfulness, or creating a peaceful environment may help mitigate stress and, consequently, alleviate back pain.

People who were taught the Smart C.A.L.M System learned how Chronology, in other words, Time, affected both their working environment and their management of the workforce who were suffering from low back pain. On top of that, they learned how they have to approach the matter, the links they had to build, and how to allow time for self-healing with the help of meditation.

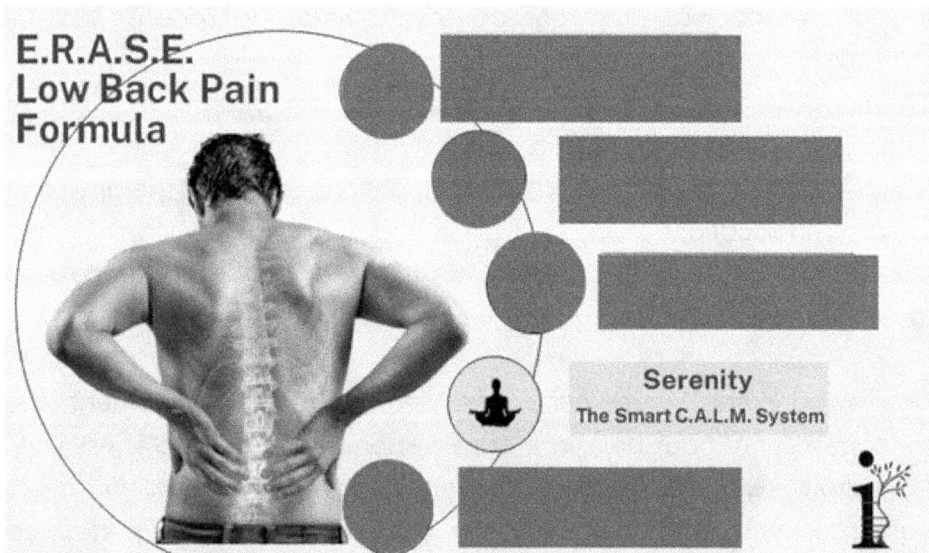

E.R.A.S.E.
Low Back Pain
Formula

Serenity

The Smart C.A.L.M. System

Time, chronology, or a timeline of a person's life can influence their lifestyle choices, including habits related to physical activity, ergonomics, and stress management. Over time, poor lifestyle choices can contribute to the development or worsening of low back pain. Adapting to a healthier lifestyle chronologically may positively impact back pain.

The chronic experience of stress over time can have long-term effects on the body, contributing to conditions such as back pain. If someone experiences prolonged periods of stress throughout their life, it may affect their musculoskeletal system, potentially leading to chronic pain issues.

It is well known that the body and mind are interconnected. The mind-body connection plays a crucial role in how stress and mental well-being impact physical health. Serenity practices, such as mindfulness and relaxation, can positively influence the mind-body connection, potentially providing relief from chronic conditions.

The chronology of one's life can impact their overall quality of life. Chronic low back pain can significantly affect an individual's quality of life, influencing daily activities and well-being. Achieving serenity and managing stress can contribute to an improved quality of life over time.

Preventive strategies can be those like embracing serenity practices and making lifestyle changes over time. They can be viewed as preventive strategies, adopting habits that reduce stress, promote mental well-being, and maintain a healthy lifestyle may help prevent or manage low back pain over the course of one's life.

In summary, the links among serenity, chronology, and low back pain lie in the potential influence of stress management, lifestyle choices, and the cumulative effects of these factors over time on an individual's physical well-being, particularly in relation to back pain.

But time can also be explained as the time spent achieving a task. Effective time management is crucial for both business success and managing low back pain in the workplace. Balancing these two aspects requires thoughtful planning and strategies to ensure productivity while prioritising the well-being of individuals dealing with low back pain. So, to have effective time management as it is linked with business and low back pain, it is necessary to prioritise tasks based on their importance and urgency. This ensures that key objectives are met while considering those that are less physically demanding during peak pain periods. Tasks have to be aligned with energy levels to maximise productivity.

The use of time blocking techniques by allocating specific time slots for focused work, meetings, and breaks and by incorporating short time for stretching and movement within the breaks to manage back pain. Optimisation and well-scheduled meetings with the goal to be concise, with clear agendas and defined outcomes, would be beneficial to a low back pain sufferer as they will be allowed for breaks and minimal periods of sitting. Tasks requiring more physical effort have to be scheduled during periods of lower discomfort.

Work can be delegated based on team members' strengths and expertise as well as when there are physically demanding tasks to be given to others, focusing on roles that align the back pain sufferer with their capabilities during episodes of pain.

To achieve clear communication channels, misunderstandings must be reduced and collaboration enhanced. These channels should include the employer, employee, as well as the team and colleagues of the back pain sufferer. Communication needs to be genuine, honest, and open, as adjustments in tasks or timelines must be set. The goals for the projects and deadlines must be realistic and achievable, considering the impact of low back pain on energy levels and physical capabilities.

The possibility of flexible work arrangements should be considered to accommodate individual preferences and enhance work-life balance. This will allow the employee to take advantage of flexible work options to manage pain. Such arrangements could include adjusted work hours or telecommuting on days of heightened discomfort.

Project management tools and communication platforms can be used to enhance efficiency and reduce physical strain.

Both employers and employees should be encouraged to prioritise self-care for overall well-being. This can be done by allocating time for self-

care activities that can alleviate back pain, such as stretching, exercise, and relaxation techniques.

Employers will be advised to implement workplace wellness programmes to promote employee health and ask their workforce to actively participate in these programmes, providing resources and support for managing and preventing low back pain. Certification could also be advisable so that there will be proof that the employee had participated, and the programme was followed.

It will be important to delve into Jenna's story. She was a senior manager in a construction company. She was very proud of her position and very ambitious as a woman in a male world. She set aggressive targets and drove her team towards success. But she ignored that the job was physically demanding and there was a risk of employees experiencing low back pain. When the first symptoms appeared, she tried to push them back in her mind, thinking that their pain was a barrier to productivity. She had a general view that these people were liars and workshy individuals. Her initial approach was to ignore their symptoms and push them to work through their condition. The whole environment was explosive. She was considered a bully because she refused to understand the root cause of her employees' struggles. This approach created unhappiness and controversy as people started to ignore her, and she saw that she was losing authority. In the meantime, the company's performance was plummeting.

She confided in me about her problems, and we worked together towards a solution.

She listened to me and learned how to take time to listen to her employees' frustrations, problems, and opinions about potential solutions. Through open and honest communication, she learned that many of her employees were experiencing pain and discomfort due to long hours of working on uneven ground, lifting heavy loads, and lack of regular breaks. Determined to make a difference, Jenna decided to implement adaptive scheduling as a solution to help her employees manage their low back pain.

As a result of her efforts, and mainly her open mind that she had developed, Jenna witnessed a remarkable transformation within her company. Employees started to listen to her and even accept her as a "pal" within their teams. Morale improved, productivity increased, and a sense of autonomy, flexibility, and harmony filled the workplace. A fair scheduling of working hours according to individual abilities was also adapted, as she wanted to accommodate her employees' needs. This way, she had not only improved their well-being but also fostered a robust, happy, and understanding team.

Her willingness to understand low back pain, her flexibility to adapt to new ideas, her ability to communicate, understand, and listen to employees' problems, her scheduling of different tasks with her team's agreement to create a fair work balance, finally increased and established the initial lost trust and created a team that thrived and led to increased productivity, as all members were enthusiastic and keen to work using their full potential.

So what did she learn?

The most important lesson was the importance of empathy, flexibility, work-life balance, trust, collaboration, and proactive approaches to addressing employee needs. By implementing adaptive scheduling, she was able to empower her employees to manage their low back pain effectively and foster a healthier, more resilient team. But the most important factors for success were an open heart, mind, and communication.

By integrating these principles into the workplace, businesses can create an environment that supports effective time management while considering the unique needs of individuals dealing with low back pain. Open communication, flexibility, and a proactive approach to well-being contribute to a balanced and productive work environment.

But to achieve a resolution of the different issues within a company, it will be necessary to approach every single one with care.

But what do I mean by saying "approach" and how is this linked with back pain? What is "approach"?

The term "approach" can be used in various contexts, and its meaning may vary depending on the field or situation. There are different general definitions of "approach," and it all depends on the context.

Generally, "approach" refers to the act of moving closer to someone or something. It can involve physical movement or a more abstract concept of getting nearer in terms of ideas, methods, or relationships. But in the context of the company, it is mainly connected with problem-solving, planning, or decision-making. "Approach" refers to a method, strategy, or systematic way of addressing or dealing with a particular task, challenge, or objective.

Using this latter term and taking approach as problem-solving, it refers to the method or strategy adopted to analyse, address, and resolve a particular challenge or issue. It encompasses the systematic steps, mindset, and actions taken by individuals, teams, or organisations when encountering difficulties or obstacles. The approach to a problem involves problem-solving techniques, decision-making processes, and the overall framework used to navigate and overcome challenges effectively. To achieve this, someone has to clearly define and understand the problem as this is the first step. This involves identifying the root cause, scope, and implications of the issue at hand, conducting a thorough analysis to understand the factors contributing to the problem. This may involve data collection, research, and assessment of relevant information and establish clear and specific goals for resolving the problem. These goals provide direction for the solution and help measure progress.

Open communication and collaboration among individuals or teams involved in addressing the problem have to be established by sharing perspectives and insights that can lead to more comprehensive solutions. These solutions can be the result of creative thinking and innovative approaches to problem-solving. This may involve exploring unconventional ideas and thinking outside traditional boundaries. These ideas have to pass through a process of identifying potential risks and challenges associated with different solutions. Understanding and managing risks are crucial for making informed decisions. Following this SWOT (Strengths, Weaknesses, Opportunities, and Threats) analysis, it will be necessary to make a well-informed decision. This includes considering the feasibility, impact, and alignment with organisational objectives. This decision has to result in a well-developed and detailed plan ready for

implementation and based on the chosen solution. It includes allocating resources, assigning responsibilities, and establishing a timeline. Regular monitoring of the implemented solution's progress and evaluation of its effectiveness has to be established. This allows for adjustments and improvements as needed. Adaptability and flexibility throughout the problem-solving process are paramount. The necessity to be open to adjusting the approach based on new information or changing circumstances.

Overall, there has to be an emphasis on continuous learning and improvement. Analysing the outcomes of problem-solving efforts provides valuable insights for future challenges.

Reflection and feedback mechanisms to gather input from stakeholders are necessary. Feedback helps assess the impact of the solution and address any unforeseen issues.

The approach to a problem is not a one-size-fits-all concept; it can vary based on the nature of the problem, organisational culture, and the specific context. A thoughtful and strategic approach is essential for effective problem resolution and organisational growth.

But what is linking the approach of tasks in a company with the low back pain-suffering personnel?

This involves designing and organising tasks in a way that considers the well-being and ergonomics of employees, particularly those dealing with low back pain. This approach recognises that the nature and organisation of tasks within a company can significantly impact the prevalence and severity of low back pain among employees.

All tasks should be designed with ergonomic principles in mind, taking into consideration the natural body movements, postures, and physical capabilities of individuals. Ergonomic modifications can include adjusting workstation height, providing supportive chairs, and optimising tools and equipment. Rotational movements during a static posture may be limited or of a short period, as they may increase the chances of low back pain. This approach ensures that employees engage in a variety of tasks throughout their workday, reducing the strain on specific muscle groups. The workloads have to be distributed evenly and consider the physical demands of tasks when assigning responsibilities. Avoiding excessive physical strain can contribute to the prevention and management of low back pain.

Regular breaks and rest periods have to be encouraged to allow employees to stretch and move around. Breaks can help alleviate muscle tension and reduce the risk of developing or exacerbating low back pain.

As mentioned previously, the necessity for the employer to provide training on proper lifting techniques, body mechanics, and postural awareness.

All tasks must be evaluated, as they may pose a higher risk of exacerbating low back pain and require modifications or redesigns. This may involve adjusting the way tasks are performed, introducing assistive technology, or incorporating tools that reduce physical strain. Employers must establish and enforce health and safety policies that prioritise employee

well-being. Ensure that guidelines and procedures are in place to promote a safe and ergonomic work environment.

Collaboration between the company and health professionals, such as occupational therapists or physiotherapists, must be established. These experts can provide insights into task design and suggest interventions to prevent and manage low back pain.

Remember Jenna's story. She took the time to listen to her employees' experiences and understand the challenges they were facing. She sought the input of experts in ergonomic design to implement changes that would support her employees' physical health in the workplace, and she witnessed a remarkable transformation within her company. She understood that empathy is essential in understanding and addressing the needs of her employees. By taking the time to listen and understand their experiences, she was able to provide the support and assistance they needed to overcome their challenges.

At the same time, she understood the importance of seeking expert opinion and input from experts in ergonomic design. Their expertise helped her implement changes that effectively supported her employees' physical health in the workplace. She learned that flexibility is important as she accommodated her employees' needs. By offering flexible work arrangements and providing ergonomic solutions, she was able to support her employees in effectively managing their low back pain.

One of the main keys was also open and transparent communication that helped to create a supportive work environment. By keeping her employees informed and involved in the process, she was able to build trust and collaboration within her team. True leadership is not just about driving results but also about empowering her team to overcome challenges and thrive. The team will push the company up. By leading with compassion and empathy, she was able to create a supportive and inclusive work environment where her employees felt valued and supported.

The valuable lessons about the importance of empathy, flexibility, communication, and empowerment in addressing the needs of her employees are paramount. By applying these lessons, she provided effective support to employees with low back pain and fostered a stronger, more resilient team.

To have a flourishing company, employees must be cared for, just as a gardener cares for his flowers. If they have rocks between their roots, he will attend to it and transplant them to fertile soil so the roots will not have any obstacles and the plants will grow without limitations.

By integrating the linking approach into the organisational culture, businesses can contribute to the well-being of their employees and create an environment that supports the prevention and management of low back pain. This approach not only benefits individuals dealing with existing back pain but also promotes a proactive and preventative mindset within the company.

Seeing this information, a new question is raised: are the approach to a problem, serenity, and low back pain linked?

Let's analyse "Link." What is the meaning of it?

In the context of serenity and low back pain, the term "link" refers to the interconnected relationship between a serene state of mind and the management or alleviation of low back pain. Serenity, often associated with a calm and peaceful mental state, can play a significant role in influencing the perception and experience of low back pain. The link between serenity and low back pain suggests that maintaining a serene mindset may contribute to the overall well-being and potentially help in coping with or reducing the impact of low back pain. This connection underscores the holistic nature of health, recognising the intricate interplay between mental and physical aspects in the context of pain management and overall wellness.

The connection between serenity and back pain involves understanding how a sense of calmness, positive connections, and supportive networks can impact the experience of low back pain. Serenity refers to a state of tranquillity and calmness. Emotional well-being, including a sense of peace and contentment, can positively influence the perception of pain. Individuals experiencing serenity may be better equipped to cope with the challenges of low back pain. So definitely there is a connection between problem-solving approaches, serenity, and low back pain. The way individuals approach and cope with problems can have a significant impact on their emotional well-being and physical health, including the experience of low back pain. To achieve this, an individual in the attempt to solve and manage their issues and challenges, including low back pain, uses coping strategies by adopting effective problem-solving skills that can contribute to a sense of control and reduce stress associated

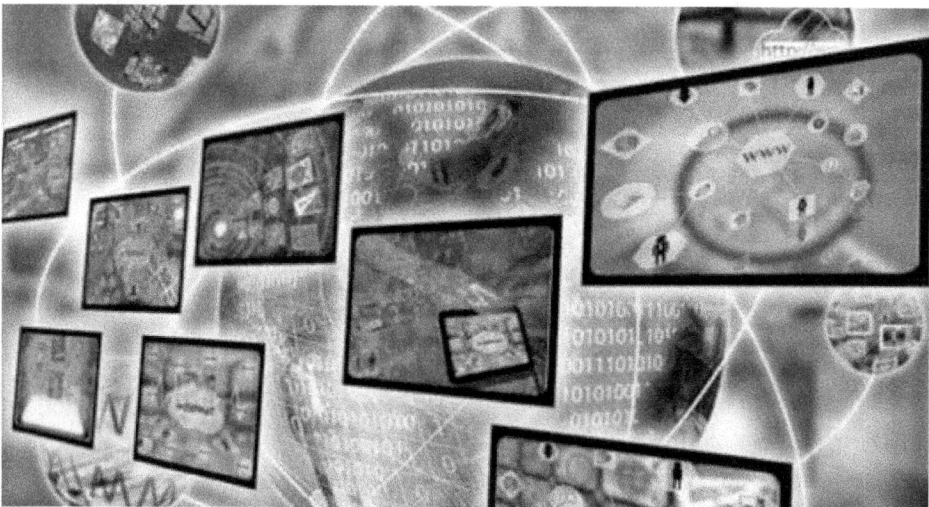

with the pain. The mindset individuals bring to problem-solving can affect their perception of low back pain. They are using a positive problem-solving mindset which may lead to a more optimistic outlook, reducing the emotional impact of pain and promoting serenity. By adapting these strategies, they create an effective problem-solving way which can help reduce stress, as stress is often linked to the exacerbation of low back pain. Serenity is closely tied to stress reduction, and individuals who approach problems calmly may experience less overall tension and discomfort.

Problem-solving approaches that focus on adaptive coping mechanisms, such as seeking social support, setting realistic goals, and breaking down complex problems into manageable steps, can contribute to a more serene response to challenges, including low back pain. Building positive links or social connections can contribute to a supportive environment. Having a strong support network, including friends, family, and colleagues, can provide emotional support, understanding, and encouragement for those dealing with back pain, promoting a sense of serenity. Open communication within social connections is crucial. When individuals with back pain can express their needs, challenges, and feelings, it fosters understanding and empathy. Feeling understood contributes to a sense of serenity, as individuals know they are not alone in their struggles. Connecting with others who have similar experiences creates a sense of community.

It's important to note that individual responses to problems and pain vary. Developing effective problem-solving skills, seeking support, and fostering a positive mindset can contribute to a more serene experience for individuals dealing with low back pain. Consulting with healthcare professionals, including pain specialists and mental health professionals, can provide personalised guidance and support in managing both the physical and emotional aspects of low back pain.

Serenity is often associated with reduced stress levels. Chronic stress can exacerbate back pain, so adopting practices and connections that contribute to serenity can indirectly alleviate some of the physical discomfort.

A positive mindset, nurtured through supportive links and serenity-promoting activities, can enhance coping mechanisms. Individuals who approach challenges with a positive outlook may experience less emotional distress.

Participating in wellness activities as a group fosters a sense of connection and shared well-being. Whether it's engaging in group exercise, yoga, or other health-promoting activities, these shared experiences contribute to a sense of serenity. Finally, integrated support systems, combining physical therapy, mental health counselling, and social support, provide a comprehensive approach. Such holistic support systems contribute to serenity by addressing various aspects of well-being.

Ultimately, the connections between serenity, links, and back pain emphasise the importance of a holistic and supportive approach to health. Nurturing positive connections, fostering a sense of calmness, and seeking support from various sources contribute to an environment that can create a positive impact.

For example, Jenna realised that by understanding and linking herself with her employees' problems and their low back pain and by implementing solutions to address them, she had not only improved their well-being but also fostered a stronger, united, and happy team.

for individuals dealing with low back pain. Consulting with healthcare professionals, including pain specialists and mental health professionals, can provide personalised guidance and support in managing both the physical and emotional aspects of low back pain.

Serenity is often associated with reduced stress levels. Chronic stress can exacerbate back pain, so adopting practices and connections that contribute to serenity can indirectly alleviate some of the physical discomfort.

A positive mindset, nurtured through supportive links and serenity-promoting activities, can enhance coping mechanisms. Individuals who approach challenges with a positive outlook may experience less emotional distress.

Participating in wellness activities as a group fosters a sense of connection and shared well-being. Whether it's engaging in group exercise, yoga, or other health-promoting activities, these shared experiences contribute to a sense of serenity. Finally, integrated support systems, combining physical therapy, mental health counselling, and social support, provide a comprehensive approach. Such holistic support systems contribute to serenity by addressing various aspects of well-being.

Ultimately, the connections between serenity, links, and back pain emphasise the importance of a holistic and supportive approach to health. Nurturing positive connections, fostering a sense of calmness, and seeking support from various sources contribute to an environment that can create a positive impact.

For example, Jenna realised that by understanding and linking herself with her employees' problems and their low back pain and by implementing solutions to address them, she had not only improved their well-being but also fostered a stronger, united, and happy team.

The key factors that played a role were learning and understanding low back pain, communicating with her workforce in an open and transforming way, becoming empathetic, and listening to their issues, providing support, and finally giving priority to preventing the causes that aggravated low back pain symptomatology.

In conclusion, she was taught some valuable lessons about the importance of empathy, prevention, communication, and leading by example in addressing the needs of her employees. By addressing their problems of low back pain and implementing solutions to remedy them, she was able to create a supportive and inclusive work environment where her employees could thrive.

Reflecting on the journey, the timeless wisdom hidden within the support she had orchestrated by placing each employee in the correct position, as a symphony conductor places each instrument accurately with the purpose of achieving ultimate harmony. She linked her employees' issues with their low back pain and found positive solutions. By leading with empathy and understanding, she managed to create a work environment where every individual could flourish, their potential soaring like the crescendo of their own symphony. She forged a bond through

their shared experiences that would continue to resonate for years to come, creating a legacy of compassion and support that would echo through the halls of her company forever.

But it will not be possible to achieve serenity without concentration within one's inner self and the attempt to improve it.

This can be achieved by means of meditation?

But what is meditation, and how can it affect or improve the management of low back pain? On top of that, how can meditation be part of life in the workplace?

Meditation is a practice that involves training the mind to focus and redirect thoughts, leading to a state of mental clarity, relaxation, and heightened awareness. It is often used as a technique for achieving a sense of inner peace, mindfulness, and overall well-being. By practicing meditation, a person can clear their mind of unhealthy, painful thoughts and replace them with peaceful ones. Meditation is widely practiced for its mental and physical health benefits.

Meditation often begins with attention on a specific point, such as the breath, a sound, or an image. This helps quiet the mind and bring awareness to the present moment.

Mindfulness is a central aspect of meditation, involving the cultivation of heightened awareness and attention to the present moment without judgment. People who practice meditation aim to observe thoughts and feelings without becoming overly attached or reactive.

By following specific breathing techniques, the promotion of relaxation and concentration can be achieved. Breath awareness is a common focal point, with attention directed to the inhalation and exhalation. This helps promote relaxation and awareness of bodily sensations.

A technique used by people who meditate is guided visualisation. This involves a facilitator or recorded audio guiding participants through a mental journey or visualisation. This can enhance relaxation and focus.

Meditation can incorporate mindful movement, such as yoga or walking meditation, but in general, it promotes awareness, allowing thoughts to come and go without judgment.

Meditation has been associated with various health benefits, including stress reduction, improved concentration, emotional well-being, and enhanced self-awareness. It is a versatile practice that can be adapted to suit individual preferences and can be done in various settings, making it accessible to people from different walks of life.

But how does meditation help with low back pain?

Meditation can be a helpful complementary approach for managing low back pain by addressing both the physical and emotional aspects of discomfort. It may contribute to the relief of low back pain by assisting in muscle relaxation and deep breathing techniques. This can help release tension in the muscles of the lower back, promoting relaxation and reducing muscle tightness and spasms associated with back pain. This way, the spine is offloaded and the pain is improved. At the same time, it emphasizes the mind-body connection. By cultivating mindfulness and awareness, individuals may become more attuned to sensations in the body, allowing them to respond to discomfort in a way that promotes relaxation and reduces the perception of pain.

Another way meditation helps is by controlling and reducing stress. Chronic stress can contribute to the exacerbation of back pain. Meditation is known for its stress-reducing effects, triggering the relaxation response and decreasing the production of stress hormones. This can lead to a reduction in muscle tension and overall stress-related impact on the back.

During meditation practice, it is observed that people keep their body in a specific posture. Maintaining good posture is crucial for preventing and alleviating low back pain. Meditation can enhance body awareness, encouraging individuals to adopt and maintain a more ergonomic posture.

Meditation teaches individuals to observe their thoughts and sensations without judgment. This non-reactive awareness can be applied to the experience of pain. By developing a mindful attitude, individuals may learn to cope with pain in a more adaptive way, reducing the emotional distress associated with it.

Meditation activates the parasympathetic nervous system, often referred to as the "rest and digest" system. This physiological response promotes relaxation, lowers heart rate, and decreases muscle tension, contributing to a state of overall calmness.

Chronic pain, including low back pain, can interfere with sleep. Meditation has been shown to improve sleep quality by reducing anxiety and promoting relaxation. Better sleep contributes to the overall well-being of individuals dealing with low back pain.

Certain meditation techniques, such as mindful movement practices like yoga, combine meditation with gentle physical activity. These practices can improve flexibility, strength, and body awareness, contributing to better management of low back pain and at the same time, improving body posture.

By focusing attention on the breath or other points of focus during meditation, it can act as a distraction from pain sensations. Shifting attention away from pain can alter the perception of discomfort, making it more manageable.

Finally, meditation helps individuals develop a non-reactive and non-judgmental mindset toward their experiences, including pain. This decreased emotional reactivity can contribute to a more serene response to low back pain, reducing stress-related exacerbations.

It's important to note that while meditation can be beneficial for many individuals, it may not be a standalone solution, and results can vary. Individuals with persistent or severe back pain should consult with healthcare professionals, including physical therapists or pain specialists, to develop a comprehensive and personalized approach to pain management. Meditation can be integrated as part of a broader strategy for promoting overall well-being and managing low back pain.

But can people meditate while at work?

Yes, people can practice meditation at work, and it can be a

valuable tool for promoting well-being, reducing stress, and enhancing focus.

How can they do it, though?

They can practice mindful breathing exercises at their desk. They can take a few minutes to focus on their breath, inhaling and exhaling slowly. This can help calm the mind and reduce stress. A person can explore different breathing techniques that can be done quietly at their desk. For example, diaphragmatic breathing, where deep inhalation into the diaphragm and slow control exhalation can help activate the relaxation response.

Alternatively, they can schedule short meditation breaks throughout the day. Even a few minutes of meditation can have a positive impact. By finding a quiet space, they can close their eyes and focus on their breath or use a guided meditation. The latter can be achieved with the use of headphones, and they can listen to guided meditations or download mindfulness applications on their phones. Many applications offer short sessions that can be done discreetly during breaks. The choice of sessions that focus on relaxation and stress reduction will be much better for the individual who chooses this way of meditation.

In case movement meditation is used, a way to incorporate gentle stretches or desk yoga into the employee's routine could be useful. This can include simple movements to release tension in the neck, shoulders, and back. By combining these movements with mindful breathing, we have a mini-meditation session. Alternatively, mindful walking practice during breaks can be another way to meditate. By taking a stroll around the office or outside, paying attention to each step and the surroundings, is a proven refreshing way to break up the workday and incorporate mindfulness.

As the talk is about breaks during them, someone can choose activities that promote relaxation and mindfulness rather than activities that may contribute to stress (e.g., checking work emails). They need to step away from their desk and engage in activities that rejuvenate their mind. In case it is a lunch break, they can practice mindful eating. They need to focus on the taste, texture, and sensations of the food. Multitasking has to be avoided, and they have to allow themselves to fully experience the act of eating.

But is meditation allowed at work?

The permissibility of meditation at work can vary depending on company policies, workplace culture, and individual job responsibilities. In many workplaces, employers recognize the benefits of promoting employee well-being and may even encourage practices like meditation to enhance focus, reduce stress, and improve overall mental health. Before implementing meditation practices at work, it's recommended to inquire about company policies, gauge the workplace culture, and communicate openly with supervisors or Human Resources representatives. If there are concerns about the acceptability of meditation during work hours, consider exploring alternative ways to incorporate mindfulness and stress reduction into your routine that align with your workplace's norms and expectations.

As noted, practicing meditation is an easy task and can be achieved using different ways. It can be a combination of music and movement or even a lack of it. The purpose is to help the mind focus and concentrate on positive thoughts and goals that everybody has. I can tell you that by taking a trip to favourite places, you may be helped and become calmer. Being calm, you can be able to follow practices that can help stay focused on a specific part and train the mind to have a positive outcome.

You can practice it in a quiet room or by listening to music indoors or outdoors. Some people prefer to be in specific spots in nature or concentrate by doing specific exercises, like yoga.

To have this desired positive effect, someone has to develop a strong belief in an idea or a desired outcome and react in a positive way in an attempt to remove any existing obstacles. Concentrating on the present goal and visualising it, while also controlling your physical reactions, is necessary. Strongly focusing on the purpose in the present moment without judgement or fear about anything you may encounter in your future life. Deep concentration within the mind itself is necessary to be achieved by using all mental and physical power to focus on that specific belief and feel in your mind that it is happening. As mentioned, in most cases, the use of soft music or a tranquil environment can help with concentration.

Meditation, though, can help with mental awareness.

This is a constant process for refining our goals; it is not a one-time process. It is something you have to repeat frequently as your circumstances change. You have to use it to clarify yourself and plan your actions. This way, you will avoid any distractions from your environment or even from your own self.

There are some steps you have to take:

**Reflection:** You need to be able to analyse the state you are in at present, pinpoint it and find out what is influencing it.

**Love yourself:** Be kind and calm with your emotions and feelings. Imagine the life you want, and you are dreaming to have and embrace it. Plan for it and live for this future "ideal but realistic" life. Fill your mind with happy emotions. If you are in a dark place and you are getting numb, you are staying there only because you are "living in the moment" and imprison yourself within it, becoming unable to come out. Do not think painful memories or fear any change. The majority of our fears are not real or useful. Become a positive person.

**Control:** Become disciplined and persist on the goals you put for yourself upon to achieve. Be able to control yourself.

"A man who cannot control self is not free" Pythagoras.  So become free.

**Flow:** Become able to create a path so well defined that the actions and thoughts will flow freely, as water flows from the river to the sea.

**Willingness:** To improve self: To achieve it you need to think with such intensity about the ideal future destination and believe in this new change you are planning for your life. Love this change, become enthused of this change, dream of this and be happy of being changed. Do not look back to the dark life. Create a strong will to improve your life one step at the time and continue progressing.

Following all of the above, you must plan, work hard, and follow the path. You have to start by establishing your present condition, and this has to be accepted.

You have to accept that back pain exists, and this is a fact. It takes time to understand and believe that back pain is there to stay, and the only thing you can do is to face it and improve the quality of your life without fear.

Depression and anxiety produced by any physical issues are recognised and accepted.

The future purpose is visualised. The pathway you need to follow in the attempt to achieve your goal has to be thought out and designed.

Aristotle was preaching that "to have a well-developed mental awareness, you need to first recognise your own feelings and be able to manage them, and secondly, to be able to recognise the feelings of your fellow humans and be able to be flexible not to offend them."

But how serenity can affect the back pain sufferers?

Serenity, especially in the context of a calm and peaceful environment, can have positive effects on individuals suffering from back pain.

It promotes stress reduction, and since stress can contribute to muscle tension and worsen back pain, a calm environment can help alleviate stress and its impact on the body.

A serene atmosphere can aid in muscle relaxation. Reduced tension in the muscles can relieve strain on the back, potentially reducing pain and discomfort.

A serene environment contributes to enhanced mental well-being. Individuals with a positive mental state may have a higher pain tolerance and cope more effectively with chronic pain conditions, including back pain. Additionally, it may promote better posture awareness. Individuals in a calm setting are more likely to pay attention to their posture, which can be crucial for preventing or managing back pain. A serene environment can stimulate the body's relaxation response, triggering physiological changes that promote relaxation and reduce muscle tension, potentially alleviating back pain symptoms.

A harmonious place can influence the body in many ways.

As mentioned earlier, there is a direct effect on the body's chemistry and the influence of hormones. Cortisol is a hormone that can create "alarm" as well as inflammation, but it has been found to be reduced following meditation and being in a calm environment. This leads to better quality sleep and reduced pain. Serenity can also contribute to the development of effective pain coping mechanisms. Individuals who experience a sense of calm may be better equipped to manage and cope with chronic pain, including back pain.

It's important to note that while serenity can be a valuable component to managing back pain, it may not be a standalone solution. Individuals with persistent or severe back pain should seek professional medical advice for a comprehensive approach to diagnosis and treatment, which may include a combination of lifestyle changes, exercises, and, if necessary, medical interventions.

Ryan is the perfect example of how meditation helped improve his company. Initially, he was a hard-core, strong-minded, driven, and results-oriented leader. He pushed his team to achieve their goals and meet tight deadlines, which were mainly his goals. When some employees experienced low back pain, Ryan found himself at a loss. He was angry and couldn't understand why they couldn't simply carry on working through their symptoms. He had experienced minimal back pain one or two times in his life after a heavy day at the gym, but this never stopped him from working. He had this false, self-oriented experience and almost demanded that everyone follow his own example towards back pain without really understanding what back pain is. He felt overwhelmed by the situation and the absenteeism and was unsure of how to solve the issue. He worried about the superiors' opinion and the impact that potential low productivity would have on the company's performance, but mainly on his own performance and future.

Following discussions, these worries were brought up and finally, he managed to change his views. He approached his employees and finally managed to make them share their daily routines and the reasons they experienced pain after certain tasks. This communication, which employees initially found difficult because they were holding back due to his previous behaviour, helped them trust him and confess the difficulties they were facing. He learned that many of his employees were experiencing stress and tension due to the working environment, and this anxiety exacerbated their low back pain. Determined to make a difference, and after research, he decided to introduce meditation as a tool to help his employees manage their stress and alleviate their pain. He managed to secure a space within the company, and during lunch break, meditation classes were introduced. The result was astonishing. He witnessed a remarkable transformation within his company. People were joyful, enthusiastic, and, above all, more relaxed. Back pain symptoms were limited, and productivity was never negatively influenced.

He had learned that communication was the key, as by taking the time to listen and understand their problems, he was able to provide the support and assistance they needed to overcome their challenges. Stress management was found to help alleviate low back pain. The introduction of meditation as a tool to help his employees manage their stress was paramount to tension reduction and the promotion of relaxation, which, in turn, helped alleviate their pain.

He learned that low back pain requires a dual approach that considers both physical and mental well-being. By incorporating meditation into his employees' wellness program, he was able to address the root causes of their pain and promote overall health and wellness.

Addressing stress and anxiety through meditation helped the workforce to develop resilience and adaptability, enabling them to cope with stressors more effectively and reduce the impact of low back pain on their lives. This created a positive working environment, which he found is essential for employee well-being and performance. By allowing meditation and promoting a culture of mindfulness and self-care, he created a supportive and inclusive workplace where his employees could thrive.

So, he learned valuable lessons about the importance of meditation and how empathy, stress management, performance, and a positive work environment are affected by such practice. By allowing meditation, he was able to empower his employees to manage their low back pain effectively and foster a healthier, calmer, and more enthusiastic team.

In our comprehensive exploration of the factors of the Smart C.A.L.M. System (Chronology, Approach, Link, and Meditation) and their profound influence on back pain within the workplace, a cohesive narrative unfolds—one that underscores the significance of mindful strategies in shaping both individual well-being and the broader work environment. As we conclude this analysis, it is evident that embracing a thoughtful chronology, adopting a mindful approach, recognising the links between various elements, and incorporating meditation practices can collectively contribute to a workplace culture that not only addresses back pain but also fosters a positive and resilient professional atmosphere.

Our examination of chronology underscores the importance of time management and the sequencing of tasks in relation to back pain. A

mindful chronology recognises the natural rhythms of productivity and fatigue, allowing for strategic planning that minimises prolonged periods of inactivity or intense work demands. This approach not only aids in preventing back pain but also promotes sustainable productivity and employee well-being over time.

A mindful approach to back health involves adopting ergonomic practices, maintaining good posture, and being attuned to the physical demands of tasks. This approach is proactive, emphasizing prevention rather than reaction to back pain issues. By cultivating a mindful approach, individuals can navigate their work responsibilities with greater awareness, reducing the risk of strain and discomfort associated with poor ergonomic practices.

The concept of link in our exploration refers to recognising the interconnectedness between various elements, such as mental well-being, work practices, and the experience of back pain. Understanding these links allows for a more holistic approach to health and productivity. By acknowledging the relationship between different factors, individuals and organizations can implement targeted strategies that address the root causes of back pain and contribute to overall well-being.

Meditation emerges as a powerful practice that contributes to serenity and plays a pivotal role in managing back pain. Mindful meditation techniques promote relaxation, reduce stress, and enhance mental resilience. This not only positively influences the perception of pain but also fosters a serene mindset that can contribute to a more positive and harmonious workplace culture.

The integration of mindful strategies—chronology, approach, link, and meditation—brings into the workplace fabric a myriad of benefits. Reduced instances of back pain, increased employee satisfaction, enhanced productivity, and a positive organisational culture are among the outcomes. By recognising the interplay between these factors and back health, workplaces can create an environment that not only prevents and manages back pain but also nurtures the physical, mental, and emotional well-being of their employees.

In conclusion, our exploration advocates for a shift towards mindful practices in the workplace—a transition from reactive measures to proactive strategies that prioritise the holistic well-being of individuals. By embracing mindful chronology, adopting a thoughtful approach, acknowledging the links between various elements, and incorporating meditation practices, workplaces can cultivate an environment where individuals not only thrive professionally but also experience a profound sense of serenity and resilience. The benefits extend far beyond the workplace, shaping a society where holistic health is championed, and people are empowered to lead fulfilling and resilient lives.

The most important gems people, and mainly leaders, have to carry in their attempt to achieve serenity are empathy, stress management, empowerment, and a positive work environment. This way, they will become caring people trusted by their employees and will drive the business to extreme heights as everybody will be behind their leader, supporting them as they supported their workforce.

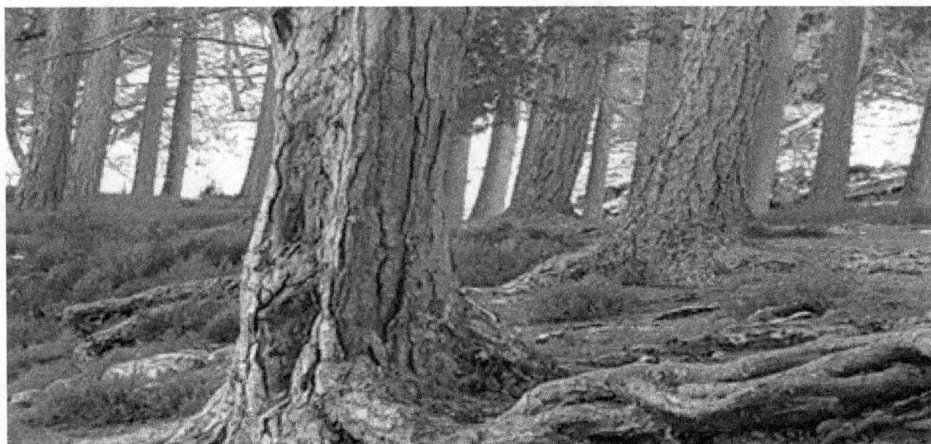

# 5

## CHAPTER

# EQUILIBRIUM

The next part of the equation that will analyse the management of back pain within a business/company is the EQUILIBRIUM.

But what I mean by that, what is it, and how is it involved with Low Back Pain management?

Scientifically, equilibrium refers to a state of balance or stability in a system where opposing forces or factors are evenly matched, and there is no net change. In various fields, the concept of equilibrium is used to describe a point at which the system is in a state of rest or uniform motion. The concept of equilibrium is fundamental in understanding and analysing systems across various disciplines, helping to predict and explain their behaviour under different conditions.

But what is the link with businesses? How does that link with back pain?

In the present, it represents the balance between Working and Social life. In our fast-paced and interconnected world, individuals often find themselves entangled in the delicate dance between professional responsibilities and the desire for a fulfilling social life. Striking the right balance between work and social engagements has become a significant challenge, as the demands of one realm can sometimes encroach upon the other. But let's explore the importance of achieving equilibrium between work and social life, the potential consequences of imbalance, and practical strategies for maintaining a harmonious coexistence.

Balancing work and social life is crucial for holistic well-being and overall life satisfaction. While professional pursuits contribute to financial stability and personal growth, social interactions foster emotional support, mental well-being, and a sense of belonging. Achieving equilibrium between these two aspects enhances not only individual happiness but also productivity and creativity in the professional sphere. It is reported in research that when employees were asked if they would work for more money or for balance in their life, 60% voted for balance.

Failure to strike a balance between work and social life can lead to detrimental consequences for individuals and, by extension, the organisations they work for. Burnout, stress, and diminished job satisfaction are common outcomes of excessive work commitments. On the social front, isolation, strained relationships, and feelings of loneliness may arise, negatively impacting mental health and overall quality of life.

Paradoxically, an excessive focus on work without adequate social engagement may lead to diminishing returns in terms of productivity. Studies consistently show that individuals who maintain a healthy work-life balance are more focused, creative, and efficient. Companies that apply this rule are more productive than others by 58%.

Regular social interactions provide a necessary break, fostering rejuvenation and mental clarity, ultimately contributing to enhanced performance in professional endeavours.

But how can that be achieved?
Initially, prioritisation and clear definition between working hours and social life have to be in place, and management has to commit to them. Priorities have to be set, and tasks that truly matter have to be identified, allowing for a more efficient use of time. This time has to be well managed and utilised correctly and efficiently. To manage this, the hours at work have to be optimised in a way that both companies and employees do not suffer. This includes prioritising tasks, avoiding multitasking, and implementing the Pomodoro Technique to maintain focus and avoid burnout.

But what is this technique?

The Pomodoro Technique is a time management method developed by Francesco Cirillo in the late 1980s. The technique is named after the Italian word for "tomato" (Pomodoro = tomato) because Cirillo initially used a kitchen timer shaped like a tomato to track his work intervals. It is designed to improve focus, productivity, and time management by breaking work into intervals, traditionally 25 minutes in length, separated by short breaks.

But how does this work and how is it implemented?

A specific task or project that needs to be worked on is selected. The timer is set for 25 minutes (this is one "Pomodoro" or work interval). This short, focused time period is known as a "Pomodoro." The employee has to work on the chosen task with full concentration until the timer rings. When the timer rings, a short break (usually around 5 minutes) is taken. During this time, the worker is allowed to stretch, relax, or do something unrelated to work. After completing a Pomodoro and taking a break, the person can choose to start another Pomodoro session. After completing four "Pomodori," a longer break of around 15–30 minutes is taken.

But what are the principles of this technique?

They include time blocking as a way of breaking the work into focused intervals that helps prevent burnout and maintains a sense of urgency. The regular breaks help maintain sustained focus and prevent mental fatigue. After each Pomodoro, the progress is assessed, and the plan is adjusted if necessary. During a Pomodoro, the focus is solely on the chosen task, and distractions are minimised.

Many people find the Pomodoro Technique helpful for managing their time effectively and maintaining productivity. However, it's important to adapt the technique to suit individual preferences and the nature of the tasks being performed.

Furthermore, a balance can be achieved by scheduling regular social activities or outings with friends and family. A network of supportive relationships can be established to provide a healthy counterbalance to work-related stress.

Time is efficiently organised with the utilisation of technology, but it is necessary to use it mindfully. While technology facilitates work efficiency, it can also blur the boundaries between professional and personal life. Limits on checking work emails or messages during non-work hours need to be placed to preserve personal time.

Finally, a person needs to be allowed to invest in self-care activities such as exercise, adequate sleep, and hobbies when they are not working. These activities contribute to overall well-being and can act as a buffer against the stresses of both work and social life.

Therefore, achieving a harmonious balance between work and social life is a dynamic and ongoing process. Recognising the importance of this equilibrium is the first step towards creating a fulfilling and sustainable lifestyle. By implementing thoughtful strategies and setting intentional boundaries, individuals can navigate the complexities of modern life, fostering a sense of satisfaction, well-being, and achievement in both their professional and social spheres.

How can low back pain sufferers achieve a balance between work and social life? What benefits does the company gain from it?

In the modern workplace, acknowledging and addressing the diverse needs of employees is not only a moral imperative but also a strategic business decision. Supporting individuals who suffer from low back pain in achieving a balance between their work and social lives not only contributes to the well-being of the employees but also offers several tangible benefits to the company. Balancing work and social life for individuals experiencing low back pain can be challenging, but it is essential for maintaining overall well-being.

Some of the advantages a business has when equilibrium is achieved are already mentioned as increased productivity. On top of that, as in every company according to statistics, there are approximately 16% of employees who are suffering from back pain. It will be beneficial for that business to proactively support employees dealing with low back pain.

By offering support and accommodations for individuals with low back pain, companies can help minimise the impact of pain on work performance. This can lead to increased productivity as employees are better able to focus on their tasks without the distraction of chronic discomfort.

It is known that chronic pain, including low back pain, often contributes to absenteeism and can be a factor in employee turnover. Supporting individuals in managing their pain and achieving work-life balance can lead to a reduction in absenteeism and staff turnover, saving the company recruitment and training costs. When companies demonstrate a commitment to the well-being of their employees, they foster a positive work culture. Supporting individuals with low back pain creates an environment where employees feel valued and cared for, leading to higher morale and increased engagement in their work.

In addition, companies that prioritise employee well-being and work-life balance can become more attractive to prospective employees. Talented individuals often seek employers who demonstrate a genuine commitment to creating a supportive and inclusive workplace. This has a positive impact on their reputation as corporate social responsibility and a commitment to employee welfare contribute positively to the company's reputation. Customers, clients, and business partners are increasingly conscious of the social values of the companies they associate with, and a supportive workplace culture can enhance the overall image of the organisation. Organisations that recognise and accommodate the needs of employees with health conditions, including low back pain, contribute to a more inclusive workforce. This diversity can lead to a broader range of perspectives and ideas, fostering innovation within the company.

In some cases, there are legal obligations for companies to provide reasonable accommodations for employees with disabilities, including chronic pain conditions. Complying with these regulations not only avoids legal complications but also demonstrates a commitment to ethical business practices.

So, supporting employees who suffer from low back pain to achieve a balance between their working and social lives is not just a compassionate approach; it is a strategic investment for companies. The benefits extend beyond the individual employees to positively impact productivity, employee morale, and the overall reputation of the organisation. By fostering a supportive and inclusive workplace, companies not only enhance their bottom line but also contribute to the well-being and satisfaction of their most valuable asset — their employees.

E.R.A.S.E.
Low Back Pain
Formula

Equilibrium
S.W.I.F.T. Stable Solution

To achieve this, it is necessary to analyse the S.W.I.F.T. Stable Solution. As this is an acronym, every letter represents an entity. These entities are Schedule, Wellness, Impact, Firmness, and Technology.

First is Schedule. But what do I mean by that?

Schedule is defined as the plan or timetable that outlines the sequential order and timing of events, activities, or tasks over a specified period. It serves as a systematic and organised arrangement of planned activities, helping individuals or organisations manage their time efficiently. Schedules are commonly used in various contexts, such as work, education, sports, and personal life, to allocate time, set priorities, and ensure that tasks are completed in a timely manner. They can be daily, weekly, monthly, or even long-term, providing a structured framework to help individuals stay organised and meet their objectives.

How then can schedule be applied for the employees and how will they be able to find the balance between work and home life?

In this modern life, finding a balance between work commitments and a fulfilling social life can be a daunting challenge. However, one powerful tool that can contribute significantly to achieving equilibrium is a well-crafted schedule.

The delicate balance between work responsibilities and a satisfying social life is a challenge for many individuals, and this struggle becomes even more pronounced for employees coping with chronic back pain. The creation and adherence to a thoughtfully crafted schedule can be a powerful strategy in achieving equilibrium, addressing the unique needs and challenges faced by employees dealing with back pain. So let's explore how scheduling can serve as a valuable tool in maintaining a balance between work commitments and social well-being for individuals managing back pain.

First, structured working hours have to be established. This will provide employees with a clear framework for their professional responsibilities. For individuals with back pain, having designated work periods helps them in managing energy levels and preventing overexertion. Within the schedule, strategic breaks need to be included. By incorporating scheduled breaks into the workday, people suffering from low back pain are allowed to stretch or move, helping them alleviate stiffness and reduce the risk of exacerbating back pain during prolonged periods of sitting or standing.

Time has to be given for either checking the equipment they use to ensure compliance with ergonomic regulations or going to appointments for health check-ups or therapy sessions. Such an organised schedule enables individuals to plan and allocate time for these appointments without disrupting their work or social commitments, promoting proactive health management.

Scheduling also helps employees prioritise tasks based on urgency and importance. By organising responsibilities, individuals can focus on high-priority work during periods of optimal energy and reserve lower-energy times for less demanding tasks, maintaining a sustainable workflow.

Allocating specific time slots for social interactions outside of work allows employees to maintain relationships and participate in activities they enjoy. Integrating scheduled time for exercise or physical therapy is crucial for individuals with back pain. Whether it's a short daily walk, stretching routine, or specialised exercises, incorporating these activities into the schedule contributes to overall back health. This intentional scheduling ensures that social engagements do not take a back seat to work obligations.

A well-organised schedule reduces the stress associated with unpredictability. For employees managing back pain, knowing when to expect work responsibilities and when to engage in social or self-care activities provides a sense of control, introduces harmony and serenity, as it helps to mitigate stress and anxiety.

So, scheduling plays a pivotal role in establishing equilibrium for employees dealing with back pain. It provides a structured framework for managing work responsibilities, incorporating necessary breaks and ergonomic considerations, and prioritising social and self-care activities. By adhering to a thoughtful schedule, employees with back pain can navigate the demands of both their professional and personal lives more effectively, fostering a sense of balance, well-being, and increased overall satisfaction.

However, it is not only scheduling that will help balance the two lives employees have.

Analysing wellness now, there is a need to see both sides: work and home life.

But what is wellness and how does it affect the back pain sufferer within a company?

Wellness refers to the state of overall health and well-being, encompassing various dimensions of an individual's life. It goes beyond the absence of illness and emphasises the pursuit of activities, choices, and lifestyles that lead to a state of holistic health. Wellness involves conscious efforts to enhance physical, mental, emotional, social, and even spiritual aspects of life.

Analytically, if the different categories are examined, it will be found that in Physical Wellness, someone focuses on maintaining a healthy body through regular exercise, proper nutrition, adequate sleep, and other health-promoting behaviours.

Mental wellness encompasses emotional and psychological well-being. It involves managing stress, fostering resilience, cultivating positive emotions, and maintaining cognitive health.

As aforementioned, Emotional well-being involves recognising, understanding, and effectively managing one's emotions. It includes developing healthy coping mechanisms and fostering positive relationships.

In addition to the above, spiritual well-being is not necessarily tied to religious beliefs but relates to finding meaning and purpose in life. It involves exploring personal values, ethics, and a sense of connection to something greater than oneself.

As the subject evolves to the mental and spiritual elements, it may be convenient to bring it slightly down to earth and examine the intellectual well-being, which involves continuous learning, creativity, and engaging in activities that stimulate mental growth. It encourages curiosity, critical thinking, and lifelong learning.

Occupational well-being relates to finding satisfaction and fulfilment in one's work or chosen activities. It involves a balance between professional responsibilities and personal life.

Environmental well-being emphasises the importance of living in harmony with the surroundings. It involves making choices that contribute to a healthy and sustainable environment.
And finally, here is the ever necessary, social wellness. Social well-being emphasises the importance of healthy relationships, effective communication, and a sense of belonging within a community. It involves building and maintaining supportive social connections.

So, it is obvious that wellness is a dynamic and multidimensional concept, and individuals may prioritise different dimensions based on their values, goals, and life circumstances.

When in business, if there are employees with back pain, it will be necessary to maintain a balance. Maintaining equilibrium between work commitments and a fulfilling social life can be a complex endeavour, especially for employees grappling with chronic back pain. The concept of wellness becomes a pivotal tool in achieving this delicate balance. It is necessary to find out how prioritising wellness can significantly contribute to harmonising the demands of work and social life for individuals dealing with back pain.

Being in a correct mental state also means that emotions are balanced. It is found that cultivating emotional wellness involves developing resilience and effective coping mechanisms. Employees with back pain, facing the challenges of both work and personal life, can benefit from emotional well-being strategies that enable them to navigate difficulties, maintain a positive outlook, and engage more fully in social interactions.

In addition, intellectual wellness encourages continuous learning and personal growth. Employees dealing with back pain can explore adaptive work strategies, learn about ergonomic practices, and seek innovative solutions that promote a more integrated approach to work and life, minimising the impact of pain. Part of the mental aspect of analysis is the spiritual aspect of life, and I don't mean only the religious element of it. Spiritual wellness involves finding meaning and purpose in life. For individuals facing the challenges of chronic pain, connecting with a sense of purpose can provide motivation and resilience. This spiritual well-being extends to both professional pursuits and social interactions, contributing to a more balanced and fulfilling life.

Every organisation has to follow strategies, guidelines, and rules on occupational health. Focusing on occupational wellness, it is found that it allows individuals to assess their work-life balance and find satisfaction in their chosen activities. Employees with back pain may benefit.

From workplace accommodations, flexible schedules, or adjustments that align with their occupational well-being, ensuring a sustainable equilibrium between work and social life.

Finally, in broad examining grounds, it is found that it is necessary to look after the social life. Prioritising social wellness involves building and maintaining supportive social connections. For back pain sufferers, having a network of understanding colleagues and friends can provide emotional support and encouragement. Social wellness fosters a sense of belonging, which is essential for navigating both work and social environments.

In conclusion, the pursuit of wellness is integral to achieving equilibrium for employees grappling with back pain. By emphasising physical, mental, emotional, social, intellectual, occupational, and spiritual wellness, individuals can create a foundation for managing pain, navigating work responsibilities, and engaging in a satisfying social life. Wellness becomes a guiding principle, offering not only relief from back pain but also a holistic approach to a balanced and meaningful existence. As organisations recognise and support the wellness needs of employees, the path to achieving equilibrium between work and social life for those with back pain becomes not only feasible but also enriching.

It is clear that back pain is influencing the balance between work and social life, but what is the impact on the companies?

So, it is necessary to explore this impact.

What is the meaning of it, though?

The scientific term for the word "impact" has various meanings depending on the context in which it is used. Here are a few common definitions:

In a physical sense, impact refers to the forceful contact or collision between two objects. For example, the impact of a hammer hitting a nail or the impact of a car crash.

In a more abstract sense, impact can refer to an emotional or psychological effect. For instance, the impact of a traumatic event on an individual's mental health or the impact of positive feedback on motivation.

Impact can also denote the outcome or result of an action or event.

This usage emphasises the tangible consequences or end product. For example, the impact of research studies on a particular field or the impact of a project on organizational success.

In discussions about the environment, impact often refers to the consequences of human activities on ecosystems, wildlife, and natural resources. For instance, there is a possible examination of the impact from deforestation on biodiversity or the impact of pollution on air quality.

"Impact" is often used to describe the influence or effect that one thing has on another. In this context, it refers to the ability of an action, event, or phenomenon to produce changes or consequences. For instance, the impact of a new policy on the economy or the impact of technology on society.

It can signify a noticeable effect on a person, thing, or situation. For example, the impact of a powerful speech on the audience or the impact of a decision on an individual's life.

In summary, "impact" is a versatile term that can encompass physical force, influence, noticeable effects, emotional consequences, outcomes, or environmental implications, depending on the context in which it is used.

In the present, though, the impact is a condition that has on the function of the human body and also on the operation of a business.

Low back pain is a prevalent and often debilitating health issue that extends its influence beyond individual suffering to cast a substantial impact on the workforce at large. It can have significant and widespread impacts on the workforce, affecting both individual employees and organisations as a whole. These impacts can manifest in various ways, influencing productivity, absenteeism, healthcare costs, and overall well-being. Here we will examine the multifaceted consequences of low back pain on employees and the broader implications for organisations, productivity, and overall workplace well-being.

But let's examine Firmness.

What is Firmness?
In general terms Firmness refers to the state of being solid, stable, or resistant to pressure. In various contexts, firmness can

describe the texture, consistency, or strength of an object or substance. Firmness can also denote strength or stability. For example, a firm grip indicates a strong and secure hold on an object, while firm muscles suggest good tone and resistance to pressure. Assessing firmness is essential in various contexts, such as in evaluating the quality of a condition or physically in relation to muscle tone or tissue texture.

But how is this linked with the balance between working and social life and, in addition, to employees suffering from low back pain?

In today's world, achieving a balance between working and social life has become increasingly challenging. This equilibrium is not only crucial for overall well-being but also plays a significant role in managing conditions like low back pain. By exploring the interconnectedness between equilibrium, firmness, and low back pain sufferers, we will highlight how maintaining firmness in both physical and social aspects can contribute to a healthier balance and alleviate the challenges faced by individuals with low back pain.

Achieving equilibrium between working and social life entails finding a harmonious balance that allows individuals to meet their professional responsibilities while also nurturing personal relationships and engaging in leisure activities. This equilibrium is essential for overall happiness, satisfaction, and fulfilment in life.

Firmness, in the context of physical well-being, refers to the strength, resilience, and stability of the body, particularly concerning musculoskeletal health. Maintaining firmness in the spine and supporting muscles is crucial for preventing and managing low back pain. Similarly, firmness in social aspects pertains to the strength and stability of interpersonal relationships, social connections, and support networks.

Individuals with low back pain often struggle to maintain equilibrium between working and social life due to the challenges posed by their condition. Low back pain can compromise physical firmness, leading to muscle weakness, instability, and discomfort, which in turn affects the ability to perform daily activities and engage in social interactions. Furthermore, the psychological impact of chronic pain can strain social relationships, contributing to feelings of isolation and loneliness.

However, by prioritising firmness in both physical and social aspects, individuals with low back pain can enhance their ability to achieve equilibrium between working and social life. Physical firmness can be promoted through exercises, ergonomic adjustments, and lifestyle modifications aimed at strengthening the muscles supporting the spine and improving posture. Similarly, cultivating firmness in social connections involves nurturing supportive relationships, seeking understanding and empathy from colleagues and friends, and engaging in activities that promote social well-being.

Maintaining equilibrium and firmness not only alleviates the challenges faced by low back pain sufferers but also offers numerous benefits for their overall well-being. By achieving a balance between working and social life, individuals with low back pain can experience reduced stress levels, improved mood, enhanced self-esteem, and better coping mechanisms for managing pain. Additionally, firmness in physical and social aspects promotes resilience, adaptability, and a sense of empowerment, helping individuals to navigate the challenges of living with low back pain more effectively.

The interconnection of equilibrium, firmness, and low back pain sufferers highlights the importance of addressing both the physical and social aspects of well-being in managing this condition. By prioritising firmness in physical health and fostering supportive social.

connections, individuals with low back pain can achieve a healthier balance between working and social life, leading to improved overall quality of life and well-being. It is essential for individuals, employers, and society as a whole to recognise and support efforts to promote equilibrium and firmness for low back pain sufferers, thereby creating inclusive environments that prioritise holistic well-being.

But do businesses benefit from this?

Achieving equilibrium between working and social life is essential for overall well-being, particularly for individuals grappling with conditions like low back pain. But how can businesses benefit from supporting their employees in maintaining this balance and addressing the challenges associated with low back pain?

Equilibrium between working and social life involves finding a balance that promotes physical and mental well-being. For individuals with low back pain, maintaining firmness in both physical and social aspects is crucial. Physical firmness entails strengthening the muscles supporting the spine, improving posture, and reducing the risk of exacerbating low back pain. Social firmness involves fostering supportive relationships, seeking understanding from colleagues, and engaging in activities that promote social well-being, all of which contribute to better coping mechanisms and improved overall quality of life.

The link between equilibrium, firmness, and low back pain management lies in the mutual reinforcement of these elements. Individuals with low back pain who achieve equilibrium between working and social life through firmness in physical and social aspects experience reduced stress levels, enhanced mood, and improved resilience to manage their condition effectively. Conversely, disruptions in equilibrium or a lack of firmness can exacerbate low back pain symptoms, leading to decreased productivity, absenteeism, and reduced job satisfaction.

Businesses stand to benefit significantly from supporting their employees in achieving equilibrium and firmness, particularly those dealing with low back pain. By fostering a work culture that prioritizes employee well-being and provides resources for managing low back pain, businesses can experience several advantages:

Employees who feel supported in managing their low back pain are more likely to remain productive and engaged at work, leading to improved overall productivity and performance.

- By promoting firmness in physical health and offering accommodations for employees with low back pain, businesses can minimise absenteeism due to pain-related issues, reducing disruptions to workflow and operations.

Creating an environment that supports equilibrium and firmness fosters loyalty and commitment among employees, leading to higher retention rates and reduced turnover costs for businesses.

Businesses that prioritise employee well-being and demonstrate a commitment to supporting individuals with low back pain build a positive reputation as socially responsible employers, attracting top talent and enhancing brand image.

Proactive measures to support equilibrium and firmness can result in cost savings for businesses by reducing healthcare expenses associated with low back pain, as well as minimising productivity losses due to absenteeism.

The synergy between equilibrium, firmness, and low back pain management is crucial for both individuals and businesses. By supporting their employees in achieving a healthy balance between work and social life, businesses can promote physical and mental well-being, enhance productivity, and reduce costs associated with low back pain. It is imperative for businesses to recognise the value of investing in initiatives that prioritise equilibrium, firmness, and low back pain management, ultimately leading to a more resilient, engaged, and successful workforce.

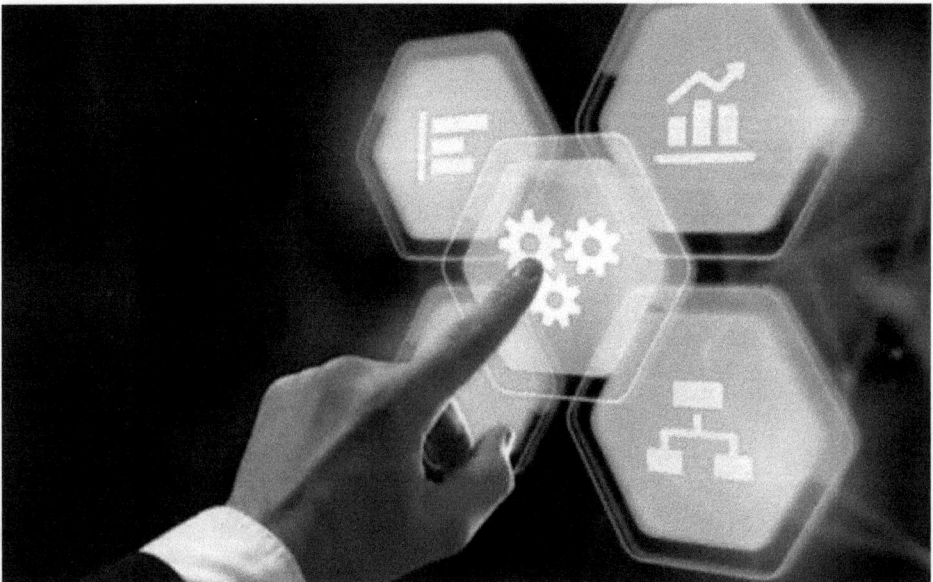

Finally, is technology the possible solution to these issues? It is mentioned multiple times that long-distance work can solve some problems.

But what is technology really?

If the term has to be defined in a blunt scientific way, technology refers to the application of scientific knowledge, skills, tools, and techniques to create, modify, and utilise tools, machines, systems, and processes to solve problems, achieve objectives, or perform specific tasks. It encompasses a broad range of innovations, methods, and devices developed to enhance human capabilities, simplify tasks, and improve efficiency in various aspects of life. Technology can manifest in different forms, including information technology, communication technology, medical technology, industrial technology, and more. It plays a crucial role in shaping the modern world, influencing how individuals interact, work, communicate, and address challenges across diverse fields and industries.

But this is not what I mean. Here it is necessary to question technology linked with back pain and the potential effects.

This kind of technology can have both positive and negative impacts on back pain, depending on how it is utilised and integrated into various aspects of life.

Technology can facilitate telehealth services, enabling individuals to consult with healthcare professionals remotely. This is especially useful for those experiencing back pain, as it provides access to medical advice without the need for frequent in-person visits.

The internet offers a wealth of information and resources related to back pain management, including exercise videos, stretching routines, and expert advice. Technology allows individuals to access these resources conveniently from their homes.

Wearable devices, such as posture correctors and activity trackers, can provide real-time feedback on body positioning and movement. This feedback can be instrumental in preventing behaviours that may contribute to back pain.

Despite these benefits, there are some negative impacts. These can be a sedentary lifestyle. The prevalence of technology, especially computers and smartphones, has contributed to a more sedentary lifestyle. Prolonged periods of sitting, often associated with the use of technology, can lead to poor posture and increased risk of back pain. Spending extended hours in front of screens, whether for work or leisure, can result in poor posture. Incorrect ergonomics and prolonged screen time may contribute to discomfort and strain on the back and neck.

Constant connectivity through technology can lead to digital overload and increased stress levels. Stress, both physical and mental, can contribute to muscle tension and exacerbate existing back pain. Technology has increased the pace and demands of many jobs. The pressure to stay constantly connected and respond to work-related communications outside of traditional working hours can contribute to stress, potentially impacting back health. The use of technology, especially handheld devices, may contribute to repetitive strain injuries. Constant texting or typing on smartphones without proper ergonomics can lead to issues such as "text neck" or carpal tunnel syndrome, which may indirectly affect the back.

The relationship between technology and back pain is multifaceted. While technology offers solutions for prevention, monitoring, and management of back pain, its overuse or improper utilization can contribute to factors that may exacerbate or cause back pain. Maintaining a balanced and mindful approach to technology use, incorporating ergonomic practices, and staying active are essential for promoting back health in the digital age.

Employers, though promoting technological progress as something that is only beneficial to the employees, actually benefit the most from it.

If we briefly analyse the influence of technology on a back pain suffering employee within the industry, we will observe that technology plays a pivotal role in shaping the dynamics between work and personal life. While offering unprecedented connectivity and efficiency, it can simultaneously influence the balance between work and social life for employees dealing with the challenges of low back pain.

Technology facilitates remote work options, enabling employees with low back pain to manage their professional responsibilities from the comfort of their homes. Remote work provides flexibility, allowing individuals to create a workspace tailored to their ergonomic needs, potentially minimizing the impact of back pain.

Digital communication tools and collaborative platforms make it easier for employees to collaborate across different time zones and locations. This flexibility in work schedules empowers individuals with low back pain to structure their work hours in a way that aligns with their energy levels and pain management strategies. Digital collaboration tools, such as video conferencing and messaging apps, facilitate seamless communication among remote teams. This not only enhances work efficiency but also fosters a sense of connection and collaboration, mitigating feelings of isolation that employees with back pain may experience.

Advancements in technology have led to the development of ergonomic solutions designed to enhance the comfort and well-being of employees.

Adjustable desks, ergonomic chairs, and voice-activated devices are examples of technological tools that can contribute to a more back-friendly work environment.

Technology offers a plethora of wellness apps and resources tailored to address specific health concerns, including low back pain. Employees can access guided exercises, meditation sessions, and personalised wellness plans, promoting self-care and proactive management of their condition. For employees seeking professional development or career advancement, technology provides flexible learning opportunities. Online courses and virtual workshops enable individuals with back pain to engage in continuous learning without the constraints of traditional classroom settings.

Social media platforms and digital communication tools facilitate social connectivity, allowing employees with low back pain to stay engaged with friends, family, and colleagues.

Advancements in technology have led to the development of ergonomic solutions designed to enhance the comfort and well-being of employees. Adjustable desks, ergonomic chairs, and voice-activated devices are examples of technological tools that can contribute to a more back-friendly work environment.

Technology offers a plethora of wellness apps and resources tailored to address specific health concerns, including low back pain. Employees can access guided exercises, meditation sessions, and personalised wellness plans, promoting self-care and proactive management of their condition.

For employees seeking professional development or career advancement, technology provides flexible learning opportunities. Online courses and virtual workshops enable individuals with back pain to engage in continuous learning without the constraints of traditional classroom settings.

Social media platforms and digital communication tools facilitate social connectivity, allowing employees with low back pain to stay engaged with friends, family, and colleagues.

Virtual social interactions provide an avenue for maintaining relationships, especially during periods when in-person activities may be challenging. Technology offers various apps designed to enhance time management and organisation. Employees can use these tools to plan their work tasks, set reminders for breaks, and allocate time for social activities, aiding in the creation of a balanced and structured daily routine.

Work-life integration apps help employees manage their professional and personal commitments more effectively. These tools can assist back pain sufferers in structuring their days to accommodate work tasks, health-related activities, and social interactions, promoting a more seamless integration of work and life.

However, technology provides flexibility. It also poses the risk of blurring the boundaries between work and personal life. Employees with low back pain may find it challenging to disconnect from work-related digital platforms, potentially leading to overwork and burnout.

In conclusion, technology presents a dual-edged impact on the balance between work and social life for employees dealing with low back pain. While providing valuable tools for remote work, health management, and social connectivity, it necessitates a mindful approach to prevent the negative consequences of overreliance on digital platforms. The key lies in leveraging technology as an enabler of flexibility and well-being, allowing employees to navigate the complexities of their professional and personal lives with greater ease and resilience. Finally, technology in the business environment is a powerful enabler that can significantly influence the equilibrium between the social and working lives of employees dealing with back pain. By leveraging the right tools and approaches, organizations can create a supportive and adaptable workplace that enhances the well-being of individuals, fostering a healthier balance between professional and personal spheres.

So, in the face of persistent back pain, employees often find themselves navigating the delicate balance between professional commitments and a fulfilling social life. The key to achieving equilibrium lies in the impactful role of adaptation.

One of the fundamental aspects of achieving equilibrium for employees with back pain is the adaptation of the work environment. Employers can make essential ergonomic adjustments, providing supportive chairs, adjustable desks, or alternative workstations to minimise the physical strain associated with prolonged sitting or standing.

Adaptability extends to work schedules and arrangements. Offering flexible work hours, remote work options, or compressed workweeks allows employees with back pain to tailor their schedules to their energy levels and pain thresholds. This adaptive approach enhances work-life balance by accommodating individual needs.

Adaptation involves modifying tasks to suit the capabilities of employees dealing with back pain. Employers can encourage task delegation or restructure responsibilities to align with the strengths and limitations of each individual. This ensures that workloads are manageable and do not exacerbate the challenges posed by back pain. Open and regular communication between employees and employers is vital for adaptation. Establishing channels for feedback enables employees to express their needs, allowing for the implementation of adaptive measures. Employers can provide support based on this feedback, fostering a collaborative approach to managing work responsibilities.

Adaptation includes providing education and training on proper body mechanics, posture, and lifting techniques. This empowers employees to adopt habits that minimise the impact of back pain during work activities. Knowledge and skills acquired through education contribute to the overall adaptability of the workforce.

An adaptive work culture is crucial in creating an environment where employees feel comfortable expressing their needs. Fostering empathy and understanding among colleagues and supervisors contributes to a supportive atmosphere. This adaptive culture encourages teamwork and collaboration, promoting a positive social environment within the workplace.

Adaptation extends beyond the workplace to social settings. Employers can organise social events that accommodate the needs of employees with back pain, considering factors such as seating arrangements, accessibility, and physical activities. This adaptation ensures that social engagements are inclusive and enjoyable for all employees.

Adaptation involves empowering employees to advocate for their needs. Encouraging self-advocacy allows individuals with back pain to communicate their requirements for a balanced work and social life. This proactive approach fosters a sense of control and self-efficacy.

The impact of adaptation is transformative for employees managing back pain, contributing significantly to the equilibrium between work and social life. Employers and organisations that embrace adaptability create environments where employees can thrive despite physical challenges. By implementing adaptive measures in the workplace, fostering open communication, and cultivating a supportive culture, organisations not only address the unique needs of employees with back pain but also enhance overall well-being, productivity, and satisfaction in both professional and social spheres. The power of adaptation lies at the heart of creating a workplace and social environment where everyone can flourish, regardless of physical challenges.

In summary if a person has to strike a balance between working and social life, they need to foster a healthier and more satisfying lifestyle.

First, they need to allocate specific blocks of time to work-related tasks and social activities. By establishing clear boundaries, individuals can ensure that work does not encroach excessively on their personal time, and vice versa.

The tasks have to be prioritised based on their importance and urgency. This helps in focusing on critical work assignments during designated times while also allocating specific time slots for social engagements.

By realistically estimating the time required for work and social activities, individuals can avoid taking on more than they can handle, reducing stress and promoting a healthier lifestyle.

Short breaks are crucial for maintaining focus and productivity. These breaks provide opportunities for social interactions, whether it's a brief chat with colleagues, a phone call with a friend, or a quick coffee break.

While schedules provide structure, they should also be flexible to accommodate unexpected events or changes. This adaptability allows individuals to address last-minute work demands or seize spontaneous social opportunities without feeling overwhelmed.

All need to spend quality time with their loved ones. By blocking out specific periods for family dinners, outings with friends, or other social activities, individuals can ensure they are fully present and engaged during these moments.

Clearly defined boundaries between work and personal life must be established.

This separation is crucial for preventing burnout and maintaining mental well-being, as individuals can mentally switch off from work when they are engaged in social activities.

Incorporating self-care activities, such as exercise, meditation, or hobbies, in their life ensures that individuals prioritise their well-being. These activities contribute to a more balanced and fulfilling life, enhancing both work performance and social interactions.

People cannot just limit themselves to day-to-day activities; they can also work on their long-term planning. By setting realistic goals and milestones for both professional and personal growth, they can create a roadmap that aligns with their values and aspirations.

A well-thought-out schedule is a cornerstone in achieving equilibrium between work and social life. It provides the structure needed to manage time effectively, prioritise tasks, and create space for meaningful social interactions. By embracing a balanced schedule, they can navigate the complexities of modern life with greater ease, fostering a harmonious blend of professional success and a rich, satisfying social life.

In the analysis of the factors of schedule, wellness, impact, firmness, technology, and their profound influence on back pain within the workplace, a holistic narrative unfolds — one that emphasises the interconnected relationship between proactive strategies and the well-being of individuals in a professional setting. As we conclude this exploration, it is evident that the thoughtful scheduling of tasks, prioritising wellness initiatives, recognising the impact of various elements, embracing a firm approach, and leveraging technology can collectively contribute to a workplace culture that not only addresses back pain but also fosters a positive, adaptive, and productive professional atmosphere.

Our examination of the schedule emphasises the importance of strategic time management in relation to back pain. Mindful scheduling allows for the accommodation of breaks, postural changes, and physical activities, contributing to the prevention of back pain associated with prolonged periods of inactivity or poor ergonomics. A well-crafted schedule not only promotes back health but also enhances overall work efficiency.

The concept of wellness serves as a cornerstone in our exploration, extending beyond mere physical health. Workplace wellness initiatives encompass physical, mental, and emotional well-being, fostering an environment that supports the overall health of employees. By prioritising wellness, organisations contribute to the prevention of back pain and the cultivation of a positive and resilient workforce.

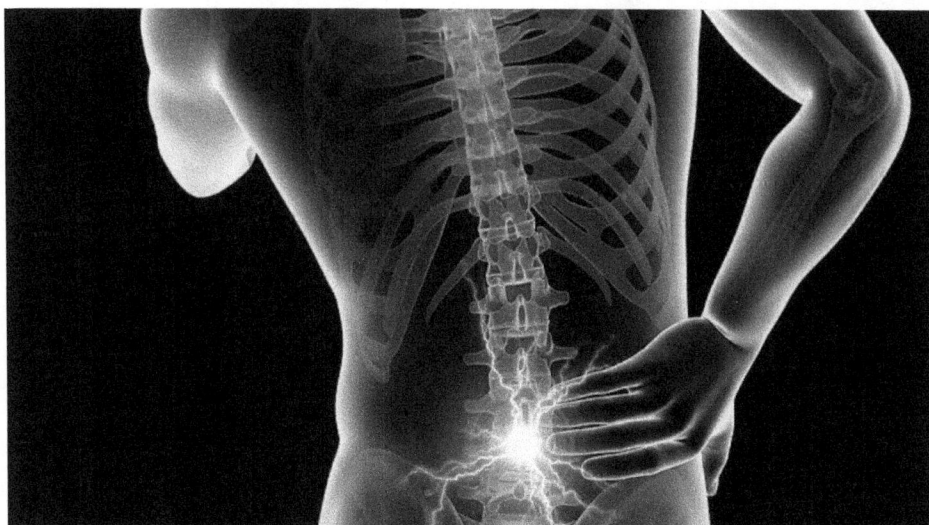

Our analysis of impact underscores the significance of recognising the consequences of various actions on back health. Whether related to physical activities, ergonomic choices, or lifestyle habits, understanding the impact on the spine is crucial. This awareness empowers individuals to make informed decisions that contribute to the prevention of back pain and the promotion of long-term spinal health.

Finally, our exploration advocates for a comprehensive and integrative approach to back health in the workplace. By embracing strategic scheduling, prioritising wellness, recognising impact, fostering firmness, and using technology, organisations can cultivate an environment where individuals not only thrive professionally but also experience a profound sense of well-being. The benefits extend far beyond the workplace, shaping a society where holistic health is championed, and all people are empowered to lead fulfilling and resilient lives.

# LOW BACK PAIN FURTHER INFORMATION IN BRIEF

## How back pain affects people.

When back pain strikes due to physical trauma or tissue damage, it affects your entire body, just like any other type of trauma. An alarm goes off in your brain as it tries to comprehend what is happening. Emergency measures

must be taken, and the disruption of various functions occurs.

The only functioning channel is self-preservation. You act like a traumatised animal, isolating yourself in a safe place, which is also a response seen in humans.

The first step is finding a safe corner and remaining silent. You don't want anyone to approach you. You don't want to move or talk; you simply want to be alone. In other words, you want to understand, analyse, and comprehend the situation in order to plan your next action.

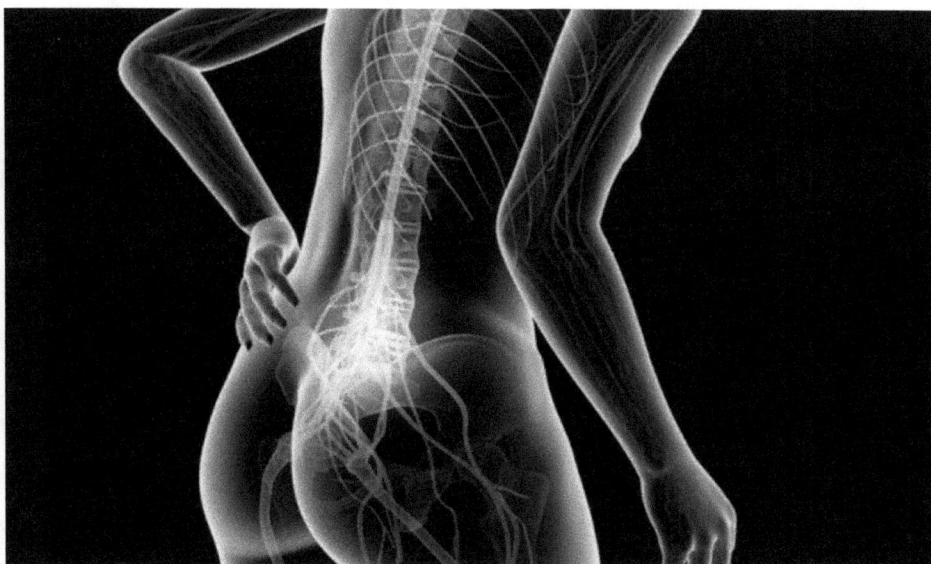

However, this is where the problem lies. Are you capable of making the correct decision and acting accordingly?

There are a number of questions that need to be answered, most of which originate from your own mind. These thoughts stem from previous painful experiences that resurface, and you attempt to make sense of them. You analyse the situation from your own perspective, which can be confusing and potentially incorrect.

Some more questions may come from your environment, your loved ones, your extended family, your friends, your co-workers, although this last group will not affect retired people.

All of them are worried about you, but their emotions are affecting you and add more confusion to the already "traumatised" brain.

Your tendency to try and isolate self is affecting others in your environment even more and there are different reactions and interactions between you and yourself, you and your immediate close family or you and the extended family as well as your friends.

Stress, anxiety, disruption of relationships, self-pity, and depression are some of the emotions that you, along with the rest of your world, are going through.

The only thing that you want from everyone, including yourself, is to be understood, informed, and supported.

Analysing my experience, I previously mentioned that the communication with people around me was disrupted. I was forced to find a solution on my own, as my doctor was not very helpful. His view that, as an Orthopaedic Surgeon, I was in a better position than him to find a solution could sound logical, but when you are suffering, you need support and possibly communication and reasoning for why you need to do one thing or another in an attempt to improve. I had none of this.

The solution had to come from me. I spent hours reading and experimenting on myself. All of this made me learn a lot about the parallel reactions we have while suffering from chronic pain, and believe me, there are a multitude of them. I will try to explain them as simply as I can.

We all know that back pain affects us in many ways. If we think logically, the original reason that initially influences us is "damage" to a tissue. This could be a soft tissue (ligament, muscle, and disc) or the bone. I am excluding back pain that originates from other organs, such as the kidneys, pancreas, vessels, etc.

This initial damage creates an initial localised reaction which, with the help of the nerves, signals the central nervous system (spinal cord and brain) by providing information. As soon as this information is received, a generalised alert goes through the body, and the words "Brace-Brace," similar to when a plane is going to crash-land, fill our system.

These results in the loss of movement due to muscle spasm as the first mechanical reaction. The rigidity of the body, as the brain forces muscles to achieve no movement, makes the muscles tired after a period of action. As the muscles overwork, they require more blood supply necessary to remove the waste they metabolically create with their constant activation. This extra blood supply creates more localised inflammation and swelling, resulting in more pressure, more pain, more painful signals sent to the brain, and more "Brace-Brace" demands.

These demands are given from the area of the hypothalamus, at the primary primitive brain, and are affecting the organs (mainly the adrenals that produce cortisol, a stress hormone) to produce the "panic attack" hormones. These hormones, in turn, affect other organs and finally the pituitary gland, which is the master gland at the base of our brain and communicates all the hormonal information to other glands as well as to the cortical brain. This is the initial vicious circle of panic.

I will now try to explain the actions and reactions that my loved ones and I went through during the course of my initial stages of back pain. You may find similarities between your story and mine, which may help you understand the reasons behind your reactions at that time.

In this personal case of mine, the following series of effects on me and my close ones were observed.

The initial injury has already been described and there were no neurological findings. I was worried about the condition and wanted answers about the cause of the pain. I was investigated by my doctor and given initial treatment, which included painkillers.

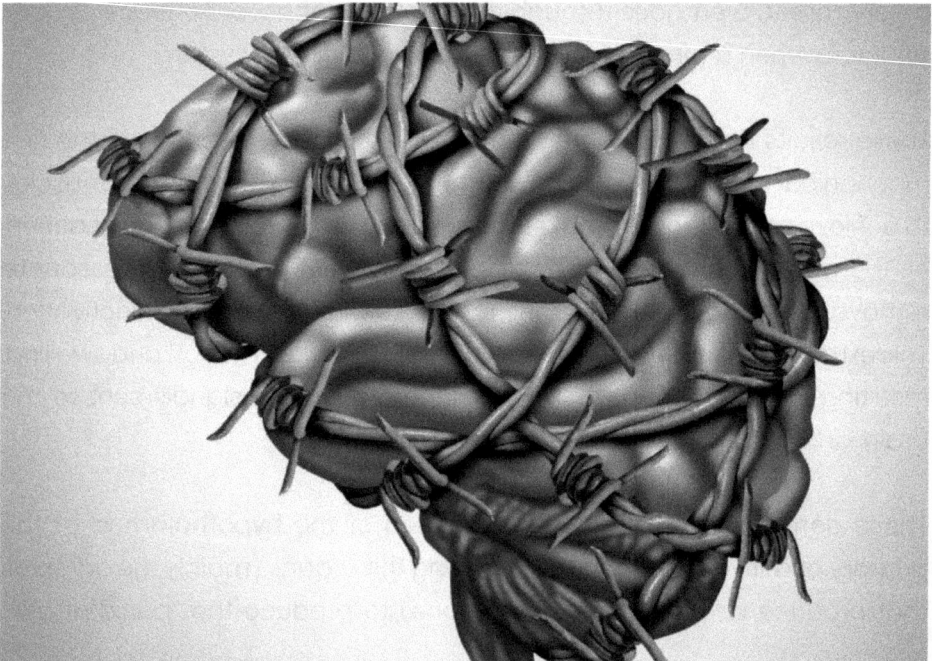

Reflecting on my condition, I noticed the different reactions and responses I had demonstrated during the initial stages of my back pain. To facilitate visual understanding, I created the following diagram.

In this first diagram, someone can see how people close to my environment started to be affected. I was keeping them at a distance, which disrupted our relationship. At the same time, I was concentrating on my tissue damage problem, which affected me. It is obvious that my concentration was initially on the back and the physical characteristics of my pain, but the focus started to shift from the structural physical anatomy to the behavioural elements of myself and the persons around me. During these initial stages, the extended family and friends were not involved. It was a "private" matter.

In the meantime, I was experiencing these symptoms, I continued studying and experimenting. Because there was no improvement, I knew that physiologically, in such cases, when time passes and the pain resolves after a period of three months, the pain is classified as chronic. The brain continues to be in a state of alert due to hormonal influence, and slowly one starts to enter into a direct relationship between pain and constant firefighting.

Studies have shown that daily mobility is affected, and this affects a person's morale. Uncertainty and anxiety slowly give way to depression, and immobility, together with depression, affects the social life of the sufferer. It is common to hear someone who is suffering say, "leave me alone". This altered social life drives the person to sleep disorder issues, family relationship problems, and so on.

Additionally, as someone goes through all these changes, it is discovered that depression, stress, and anxiety affect hormones, and further

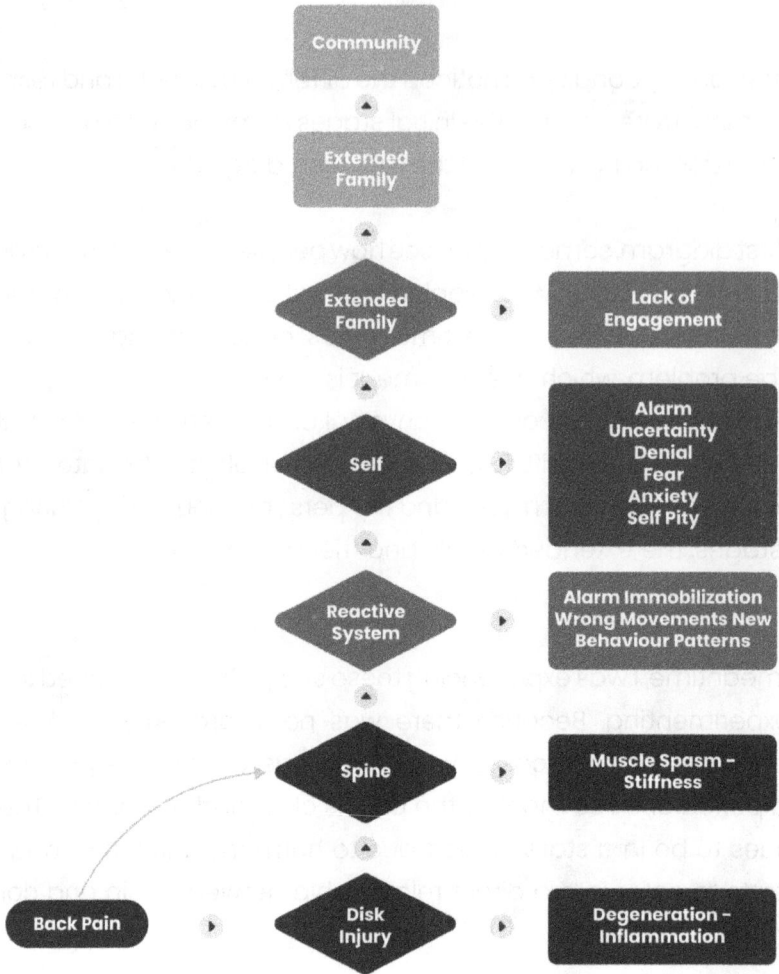

symptoms such as sleep deprivation may be added. If lack of social life is also added to all these changes, the hormonal imbalance becomes more noticeable, creating an environment for further mental and behavioural disruptive issues.

The body and mind enter a strange state of problem acceptance and go into a downward spiral that feeds the pain and depression further. This is the vicious circle of chronic pain, and it is obvious that biology plays a small but constant role, mainly due to feeding it via the emotional factors.

The unfortunate consequence is that the "disruptive" behavioural changes of the sufferer directly affect the close family, and this affects their own hormonal state, causing them to be in a "panic" condition themselves. Their emotional state becomes strained, and this sets off an emotional domino effect that eventually spreads to the wider community. This situation can create a multitude of opinions and confusion.

In the illustration above, it is clear how little space the physical "problems" occupy in comparison to the combined psychological, social, or behavioural "problems" that are affected by chronic back pain. The physical issues may be the initial presentation, but the rest are the result of the accumulation of different factors and stimuli over time.

Regarding the observations of my case, as the painkillers did not make much of a difference and I was still in pain, my attitude changed, causing further stress for everyone involved. The main impact was now visible on the people around me. These emotions were intense, and the worries were apparent due to uncertainty about my future outcome and how

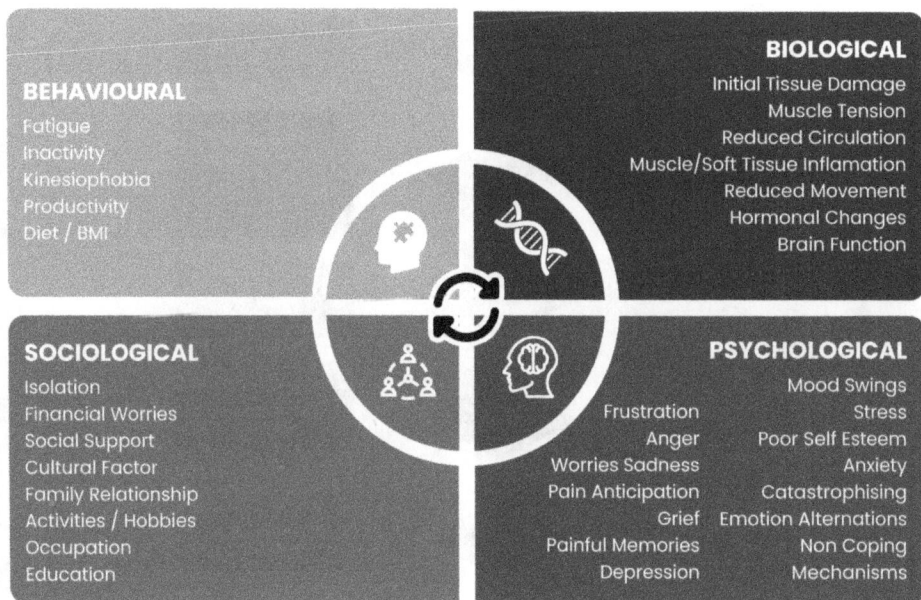

**BEHAVIOURAL**

Fatigue
Inactivity
Kinesiophobia
Productivity
Diet / BMI

**BIOLOGICAL**

Initial Tissue Damage
Muscle Tension
Reduced Circulation
Muscle/Soft Tissue Inflamation
Reduced Movement
Hormonal Changes
Brain Function

**SOCIOLOGICAL**

Isolation
Financial Worries
Social Support
Cultural Factor
Family Relationship
Activities / Hobbies
Occupation
Education

Frustration
Anger
Worries Sadness
Pain Anticipation
Grief
Painful Memories
Depression

**PSYCHOLOGICAL**

Mood Swings
Stress
Poor Self Esteem
Anxiety
Catastrophising
Emotion Alternations
Non Coping
Mechanisms

life would progress. My own emotions were not helping them at all. My weight was increasing, and I was worried, entering a stage of self-pity. Blood pressure and stamina were affected.

In the diagram above, someone can see the changes that were affecting me during this period of my life. I was completely ignoring my physical pain, and my main concern was a constant reflection on the facts that were the result of the original injury. I was constantly rehearsing the scene of the injury and how it had ruined my activities. I was angry at my doctor and the way he managed my needs. I was pitiful and constantly angry at myself; my colleague who moved at the last minute and what might happen if he wasn't there. I was angry with my doctor's attitude. I was not ready to accept the long-standing back pain. I was not a happy

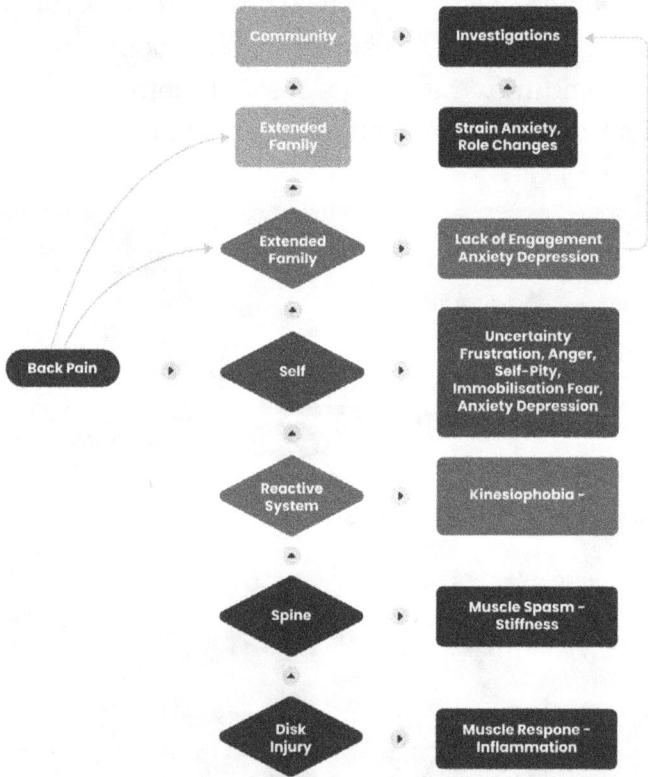

person. When my doctor finally announced my borderline diabetes and the need for constant blood pressure medication, I woke up. My belief that medications and pills had to be removed from anyone's thoughts forced me to change. An inner strength grew.

The negative reflection I had been engaging in until that time changed to positive thinking, and I started to change. Slowly, I was able to find solutions to my problems.

As soon as I found out that I was improving, I again did something that I do most of the time: further positive reflection. This self-analysis and deep thinking helped me a lot. I put myself in the positive position that I am cured, and my perspective changed the whole picture. Everyone's emotions were reversed, and I mainly started to concentrate my thoughts

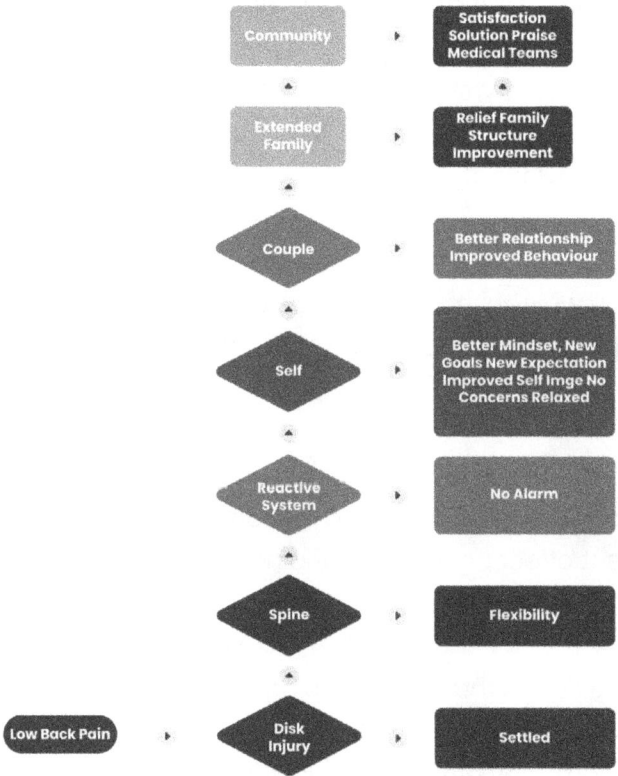

on the original problem, which was the physical/mechanical issue.

This analysis of the different stages of my symptoms gave me a potential diagnosis. As my initial pain and twisted spine improved with another accidental twist, and nothing was obvious on the original X-rays, my potential diagnosis was subluxation of the facet joints at some level of my spine. The potential future would be arthritis of the joints and possible long-term degeneration of the discs.

The diagram above shows exactly how the successful "treatment" changed the emotional picture of the loved ones. The picture of self as well as my attitude towards the back pain. It is evident words that I used; they were positive.

Based on my story coming out of this labyrinth of physical and emotional trouble you need to move to the correct direction slowly and executing this movement step by step. Analysis of the physical/biological part of the circle is necessary. The base of tissue damage with the rolling effect is leading to behaviour of constant pain.

It is already known that chronic low back pain affects more people on the planet than we can imagine and as age progresses the incidence is increasing. They find that these symptoms create loss of their energy and affect them mentally as well.

It is obvious from all the diagrams above that the emotional element is greater than any physical issues in a person suffering from low back pain. This has a direct effect on the surrounding environment and social circle, affecting the behaviour of a number of people.

This is the vicious circle that you are going through, living a life with chronic low back pain, missing family activities, and not being able to enjoy the laughter and company of your grandchildren or hobbies and other daily

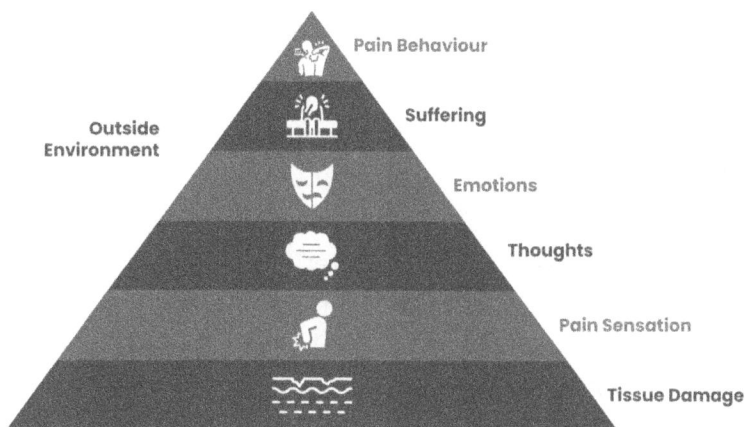

activities. This is the reason we are here together, to walk the journey of symptom management and live a life of better quality.

From my professional experience, I can tell a story of an elderly lady who walked into my consulting rooms. I had seen her in the past and had ordered X-rays. She appeared to have degenerative discs in multiple levels and was suffering from osteoporosis (thinning of the bone structure), but she had no obvious compression fracture as a result of it. After she sat in front of me, she mentioned that she feels exhausted due to her constant low back pain.

In her words, she told me:

"I find that making the bed every morning is a serious business. As I bend over to fix the sheets, I get pain in the back, and it takes me forever to get it made. The rest of the housework is torture too. I cannot even do the hoovering or lift the pot from the stove. Standing in front of the sink to wash the dishes is an adventure. I find myself sitting down most of the time or lying down in bed trying to relieve the pain. At night, I cannot sleep well. I am tired at all times. I cannot go anywhere. I lost my friends. My only activity now is to open the fridge and munch on whatever I can find inside it. I feel isolated. Thank God my son arranged for a helper to come over once a week and do the heavy cleaning, but I feel that I am useless. I don't want such a life and I pray to God to take me. I am old, I lived my life. Why do I still live? I don't know. I am debilitated physically; I am an emotional wreck and I don't know what to do. I am here to ask your opinion if you think that I need to have a trip to Switzerland to organise my voluntary exit from this life. Is it worth spending the few monies I put aside?"

Analysing this grim story and thinking deeply can lead to finding out the reasons that pushed this person to say what she said. On physical grounds, she has degeneration and osteoporosis. This is the tissue involvement. This is influencing her psychological sphere as she is worried, has poor self-esteem, she is stressed and catastrophizing, she is frustrated and angry with herself, she is mentally and physically sad, and she is expecting the daily pain to be present. Her emotional status is not normal, and she feels that she cannot cope with her condition.

The combination of the physical and emotional element is affecting her sleep, and because of it, she feels fatigued. Her diet is bad, and although she is not mentioning it, she is gaining weight. In parallel, she is isolated without friends and family, with minimal support.

Due to the combined issues she is facing, the degree of depression she is into drove her to make statements of self-destruction.

The question is if the mental status is affecting her symptoms. It is known from literature that depression and anxiety are influencing and amplifying the symptoms of chronic low back pain. Her physical and mental status collaborate and change with the constant hormonal influence they have on her central nervous system and the brain's chemistry. Pain itself is her new existence, as she believes that this is the only way she has to live her life. The pain is linked with emotions and has become engraved in her mind as the only thing that has control over her, changing her behaviour.

All the above combined are influencing her social life and the lack of it increases the anxiety as she continues to go around and around this way. The only way she thinks that she can stop this circle is to terminate her life.

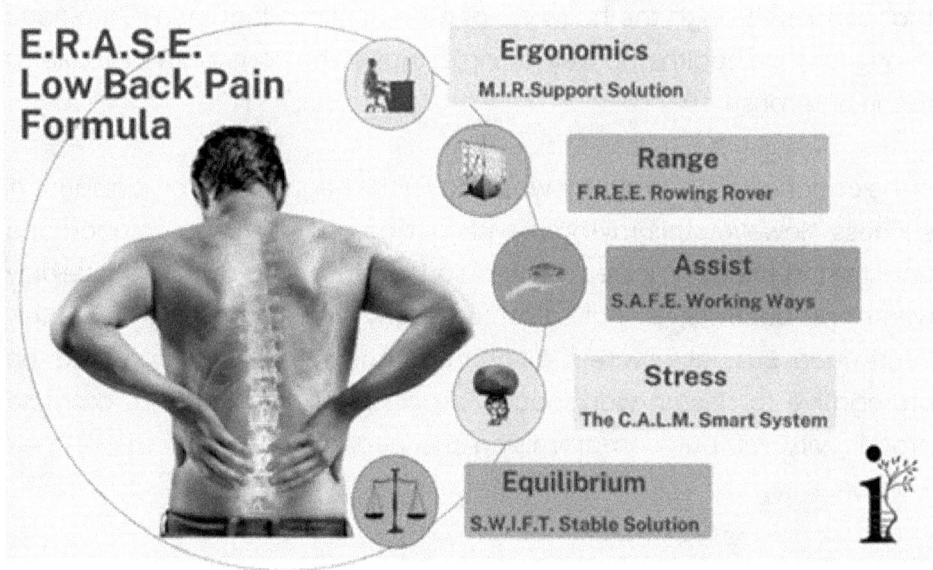

E.R.A.S.E.
Low Back Pain
Formula

Ergonomics
M.I.R.Support Solution

Range
F.R.E.E. Rowing Rover

Assist
S.A.F.E. Working Ways

Stress
The C.A.L.M. Smart System

Equilibrium
S.W.I.F.T. Stable Solution

# EPILOGUE

In the final notes of our journey through the labyrinth of low back pain management, safety, and productivity in the realm of working life, we find ourselves standing at the precipice of profound transformation. The symphony of well-being, safety, and productivity plays on and business owners emerge as conductors with the power to shape the harmonies resonating through the corridors of their organisations.

As we delved into the multifaceted dimensions of low back pain, the realisation unfurled that the well-being of employees is not a mere obligation but a cornerstone upon which the edifice of organisational success stands. The management of low back pain is not just a response to the challenges faced by individuals; it is an investment in the resilience and vitality of the entire workforce.

Safety, a virtuoso in this orchestration, takes centre stage. Business owners, akin to guardians of a sacred trust, bear the responsibility of fostering environments where employees feel shielded from the perils of occupational hazards. "Safety first" is not a mere slogan but a mantra that echoes through the hallways of conscientious leadership, a pledge to prioritise the health and well-being of those who contribute their talents to the enterprise.

In the cadence of productivity, we discover the heartbeat of organisational success. However, this rhythm needs not be one of relentless pace and unwavering intensity. Instead, it should be a dance, a dynamic interplay where productivity is not divorced from well-being but intricately intertwined. Business owners, as choreographers of this dance, hold the prerogative to design workspaces, policies, and cultures that catalyse productivity without compromising the health and happiness of their workforce.

To the business owners standing at the helm of their enterprises, consider this a guidebook, a compass navigating the uncharted waters of a new era in workplace well-being. Forge alliances with ergonomic principles, letting them guide the architecture of your workspaces. Illuminate the path with the lantern of serenity, recognising that tranquillity is not an indulgence but an essential element in the alchemy of sustained success. Embrace balance as a North Star, steering your organisation away from the extremes and towards the equilibrium where both professional pursuits and personal well-being can flourish harmoniously. Let the range of joint motion be a manifesto, inspiring movement, and flexibility in your workforce, transcending the limitations of sedentary existence.

In extending compassionate assistance to those grappling with the weight of low back pain, you become not just leaders but guardians of the human spirit within your organisation.

"The true measure of any society can be found in how it treats its most vulnerable members," said Mahatma Gandhi.

In the realm of business, your leadership is measured not just in profit margins but in the compassion and support extended to those navigating the challenges of pain.

As you navigate this complicated balance of low back pain management, safety, and productivity, remember the words of the ancient philosopher Lao Tzu: "The journey of a thousand miles begins with one step."

"The true measure of any society can be found in how it treats its most vulnerable members," said Mahatma Gandhi.
In the realm of business, your leadership is measured not just in profit margins but in the compassion and support extended to those navigating the challenges of pain.

As you navigate this complicated balance of low back pain management, safety, and productivity, remember the words of the ancient philosopher Lao Tzu: "The journey of a thousand miles begins with one step."

The path to a workplace where well-being, safety, and productivity combine may seem challenging, but every intentional step you take propels your organisation towards a brighter and more sustainable future. In the symphony of business, let the crescendo of well-being, safety, and productivity resound, creating a melody that resonates not just within the confines of your organisation but reverberates through the collective consciousness of the working world.

In the culmination of our exploration into the intricate tapestry woven by the nexus of business dynamics and the well-being of employees grappling with the burdens of low back pain, we find ourselves at a juncture where the threads of ergonomics, serenity, balance, range of joint motion, and compassionate assistance have converged to paint a portrait of profound transformation.

As we delved into the lives of individuals manoeuvring through the corridors of corporate existence, the stark reality of low back pain as a prevalent companion on this journey became apparent. Yet, through the prism of understanding, a beacon of hope emerged – a realisation that businesses hold the power not just to create thriving enterprises but also to foster environments where the flourishing of individual well-being is paramount.

Ergonomics, the silent architect of workspaces, stood as a sentinel, reminding us that the design of our surroundings profoundly influences our physical health. The embrace of ergonomic principles transcends the mere arrangement of desks and chairs; it is an affirmation that every element of our work environment can be crafted to nurture the vitality of the human body.

In the stillness of serenity, we discovered a sanctuary where the tumult of corporate life subsides, and the balm of peace is applied to the wounds of stress and tension. Through mindfulness and intentional practices, individuals and organizations can forge a path toward serenity, not merely as an escape from the demands of business but as an integral aspect of sustainable success.

Balance, the delicate equilibrium between professional pursuits and personal well-being, emerged as a linchpin in our exploration. The symphony of a harmonious life resonates not in the relentless pursuit of perfection but in this peculiar dance between career aspirations and the caring of one's physical and mental health.

The exploration of the range of joint motion served as a reminder that within the spectrum of movement lays the key to resilience. From the fluidity of mobility emerges strength, and through thoughtful exercises and considerations, the constraints of low back pain can be transcended.

So let us be architects of change, weaving a narrative where businesses and individuals coexist in a symbiotic dance, each influencing the other toward greater heights of flourishing. In the delicate interplay of ergonomics, serenity, balance, range of joint motion, and compassionate assistance, we find the melody of a healthier, more harmonious future for businesses and the individuals who comprise their beating hearts.

So, are the low back pain sufferers a burden for the companies they are working in?

There is ample evidence to suggest that low back pain sufferers can be positive and valuable members of companies, rather than burdens.

According to research, low back pain is incredibly common, affecting a significant portion of the global population and affecting them at some moment in their lives. Given its prevalence, it's likely that many employees within a company may experience low back pain at some point and this is calculated to be 16% of the workforce.

But low back pain does not diminish an individual's skills, talents, or contributions to the workplace. Many employees who experience low back pain possess valuable expertise, experience, and qualifications that make them valuable assets to their companies.

It is found that those who are suffering often develop strategies to manage their condition and continue working effectively. This adaptability demonstrates resilience and determination, traits that are highly valuable in any workplace.

Research indicates that while low back pain may temporarily affect productivity during episodes of pain, employees typically maintain or even improve their productivity over the long term. With appropriate support and accommodations, employees with low back pain can continue to make meaningful contributions to their companies. This is led by the following factors. Firstly, the loyalty of the individuals towards the company that is supporting them and also guilt as they are feeling responsible for any delays their condition caused during their absence.

People with low back pain may offer unique perspectives and insights that contribute to innovation within their companies. Their experiences navigating challenges associated with back pain may inspire creative solutions and approaches to various problems.

Embracing employees with diverse experiences, backgrounds, and abilities fosters a culture of inclusivity and diversity within companies. Such environments are often more innovative, collaborative, and successful. Providing support and accommodations for all employees can strengthen a sense of loyalty and commitment to their companies. Employees who feel valued and supported are more likely to remain with their employers long-term, reducing turnover costs and maintaining institutional knowledge.

Organisations have legal obligations to provide reasonable accommodations for employees with disabilities, including those with chronic conditions like low back pain. Failing to support these employees can lead to legal liabilities and reputational damage for companies.

In summary, low back pain sufferers are not burdens to companies; rather, they are valuable members who bring diverse skills, experiences, and perspectives to the workplace. By providing support, accommodations, and fostering inclusive environments, companies can harness the full potential of all their employees, including those with low back pain, to drive success and innovation.

"The measure of a society is found in how they treat their weakest and most helpless citizens," remarked the philosopher Pearl S. Buck.

Taking care of people in need, as well as taking care of ourselves, is the supreme gift a person can give to another human being. This will create eternal gratitude and a strong bond between these two individuals, and it is paramount to the progress of the human species.

Thank You